THE

EXECUTION

CHANNEL

A Political Fable

BY

MICHAEL MCCORD

The characters and events described in this novel are fictional.

At least the author hopes they will remain fictional.

For

Anne

Acknowledgements

Thanks to Tom Sedoric for his financial support. Thanks as well to William Duncan, Peter Miller, Dick Ingram, Tom Pearson, Kent & Sandy Comeau, Joan Jacobs & Larry Drake, and Jane & Jeff Cutter for their generous Kickstarter donations to help publish and support this book. Thanks also to Mary Johanna Brown, Matt Talbot and Crystal Paradis at Brown & Company Design in Portsmouth, NH for the creative book cover design; and to Christine French for her great editing eye.

Inspiration thanks

Jonathan Swift, Voltaire, Joseph Heller, Groucho Marx, George Orwell, Machiavelli, and Ayn Rand.

In Memoriam

We miss you Maureen

CHAPTER ONE

REAL AMERICA FIGHTS BACK

"Real men, Real Americans ignore the facts and pay homage to their gut instincts, which they know are right. I don't believe in history, I don't believe there is a real history that the liberal cowards and moocher takers would have you believe. There is no history, only the glory of Real American faith."

– GOV. LAWRENCE C. BOWIE, REAL AMERICAN REPUBLIC OF TEXAS

Once upon a time in the not-too-distant future, Gov. Lawrence C. "Demon Seed" Bowie of the Real American Republic of Texas was the most controversial and colorful politician in the not so United States of America. Many smart minds believed a bright future was assured for Bowie as much as any bright political future can be assured. But during that pivotal year of 2018, Bowie was in a political fix of his own making and he knew that not getting out of the predicament could derail his presidential aspirations and undermine his stature as undisputed leader of the Real American Party. He was also in the crosshairs of political enemies determined to short-circuit his political rise by ballot or bullet. Yet, as this tale will tell in greater detail, Bowie would solve his problems and find salvation as the founding father of the Execution Channel.

Bowie would be the first to tell you the story of the Execution Channel couldn't be understood properly without appreciating the vital role he played. In fact, it was a surprise to many that Bowie would become the author of the first, bloody draft of the Execution Channel's history. Bowie later made a fortune promoting the gospel that there was only one true story behind the Execution Channel but as you will see dear reader, there was a more substantial and complex version which has remained hidden until now.

But it is important to give Bowie his due. His emergence stunned those who treated him as a junior business partner and a very junior business partner at that. But winning the expectations game was nothing new for Bowie. It was said by people who had habitually underestimated him that he was not the brightest or most articulate politician. Even Bowie supporters were left baffled by the source of his power. "The words and ideas flowing from Bowie's mouth seem born from a distant and un-explored universe," said RAP political commentator Michael Stanbye who had watched Bowie's rise from obscurity. "He is the most danger-ous man in the country, so it's a good thing he's on our side."

Bowie was personally untroubled by criticisms of any type and seem-ingly went out of his way to invite scorn from his opponents. For exam-ple, during the infamous Texas gubernatorial primary of 2016, Bowie's top rival chose to attack Bowie's intellectual and verbal shortcomings as a surefire campaign strategy.

"It should scare us that this man was elected to Congress. Really, we should take time to investigate the sanity of those supporters in his district," said Congressman Joe Someret, who served three terms in Congress with Bowie and knew him well. "Honestly, does anyone have any clue what Bowie is saying or what inane conspiracy he will pull out of his hat? We can't be sure whether he even knows or cares what he's talking about and he makes no pretense to care about anything resem-bling the truth. Is this the man you want as governor, one who lives in fantasy land of his own making?"

When the primary began, Someret was considered the favorite because his political bona fides were beyond question. He was a very conser-vative Mad Hatter Republican with a 100 percent Liberal Hater rating from the Liberty Standard Foundation. Along with Bowie, he was one of the founding members of the Real American Party.

Bowie and his campaign returned fire and weakened Someret with a constant barrage of negative ads and systematic rumor-virus releases to the media. Bowie accused Someret of having a collective mind-set for seeking federal relief money when Someret's home city of Galveston was virtually destroyed in the Great Gulf Hurricane of 2015. Bowie accused him of dubious Galtian loyalty, of sheltering known moocher and taker activists in his family, and of being a less than enthusiastic liberal hater.

"He's an imposter. The career congressman may have a 100 percent Liberal Hater rating, but it's a front of deceit meant to subvert the Galtian Imperatives," Bowie said. Political analysts said the most devastating blow came when Bowie's campaign discovered that Someret once had paid one percent of the health insurance premiums for the employees at his balloon-making factory.

"My fellow Texans, there is nothing more subversive than a Real American Party member who talks one way and acts another by coddling the help. Can we trust a man who gives lip service to the Galtian Imperatives and then wastes his hard-earned money on an altruistic whim?" Bowie said during the most heated of their three debates. "Congressman Someret has spent too much time in the Washington cesspool acquiring the bad habits of so-called good intentions."

Someret tried to fight back. "I have no doubt that Congressman Bowie excels at professing loyalty to the Real American Party but let us be clear about this crucial fact: his utmost loyalty is to his own megalomania," Someret countered in the debate. While the audience cheered and jeered loudly and fights broke out between supporters at the college auditorium hosting the debate, Bowie counterattacked swiftly.

"Megalomania in the defense of Real America and the Galtian Imperatives is no vice, Congressman," Bowie said loudly. "Perhaps you should try it sometime."

During this most expensive campaign in state history, Bowie also attacked Someret relentlessly for being "soft on gun liberty and a friend of tyranny," for considering (but not voting for) a measure to require government background checks to purchase backyard rocket launchers and antiaircraft missile systems. "Someret wanted the government to have your name, you a law-abiding citizen exercising your constitutional right to bear arms and defend your property from the moochers and looters and invaders from the United Nations," Bowie said at a campaign stop in San Antonio. "But we know that once the government gets your name, they have you and can profile you. They can squeeze the liberty from your balls and once they squeeze the liberty from your balls, it leads to a plague of tyranny that Someret supports."

The tactics worked and Someret was easily defeated on primary day. RAP political commentators were impressed by Bowie's performance. "He has redefined what we consider the truth and positively shattered previous boundaries of political incoherence," said Henry Jenkins, a longtime Bowie watcher and commentator on the Galt News Channel. Bowie took pride in his incoherence and haphazard relationship with the truth because he had calculated that being considered not overtly smart or clearly understood had the advantage of creating confusion. "I have an efficiently uncluttered and unconfused mind and what I don't understand or when facts make me even slightly uncomfortable, I simply eliminate such clutter," Bowie told a group of wealthy financial supporters who were curious about the source of his remarkable political genius.

The Imbecile Caucus

Bowie's political pedigree was unmatched. During his three terms in Congress, Bowie emerged as the unofficial leader of the influential, 14-member House group called the 'Imbecile Caucus.' The Imbecile Caucus was a group of Mad Hatter Republicans who made daily headlines for feats of incoherence and unsubstantiated accusations. The IC, as it came to be known, was credited for setting a new standard of enlightened political discourse in Washington, D.C. by making "fact-free" statements its guiding principle. No one did it better than Bowie.

For example, Bowie drew cheers from IC members when he took to the floor of the House in 2014 and unleashed a multi-faceted broadside against what he called "the hordes of liberal traitors in the federal government" and the mainstream political party appeasers who tolerated them. "I have a list of 37 known liberals behind the secret collective mindset agenda to force their tyranny on liberty-loving Real Americans," he stated. Then he called for congressional investigations into a "secret United Nations black helicopter brigade that was colluding with an ultra-secret federal government agency to spray mind-controlling pixie dust at night and turn us into moocher zombies during the day. You can hear it here for the first time: their evil Agenda 69 is designed to restrict your rights to copulate."

As a finishing touch, Bowie also accused President Burt Octavian of funding "hidden government concentration camps run by a liberal elite cadre of feminists and homosexuals and abortionists and looters and moochers who want to brainwash law-abiding Americans into paying more taxes. We cannot allow this evil to continue and must investigate further."

Bowie didn't know or even care much if these alleged secret initiatives actually existed—his aides fed him information gleaned from one Real American Party-aligned blog site maintained by psychiatric hospital patients. He didn't mind when none of his 262 calls for congressional investigations into "widespread liberal malfeasance" led to an actual investigation. What mattered is that the lack of investigations proved the conspirators were good at keeping the truth from the people and that their conspiracies were thus true and growing by the day.

He took pride in his hit and run and hit again tactics and was adept, he said, at "keeping those liberal elitists afraid." His Imbecile Caucus colleagues credited Bowie with being the best at playing the RAP echo chamber, rumor-mongering game and for being a strong leader in bringing frequent halts to the actual work of Congress.

His constituents, "ma base" he called them, thanked him for speaking out and stopping Congress from doing more evil. Bowie's base was certain the conspiracies existed because Bowie's statements of fact were confirmed by the RAP media and blogger network that amplified his accusations back to his base. Bowie's supporters demanded more information, more talk of conspiracies and investigations, and demanded that more government officials be brought to justice.

"My job as a public servant isn't to find the truth and worry about so-called facts. My calling is to boost hysteria and promote conspiracies at every opportunity," Bowie told a columnist from the Sludge Daily War Report. "It doesn't matter whether these conspiracies are so-called true or not. What matters is that I feed the fears and prejudices of my base. They have asked for this menu and they deserve nothing less."

Even when an editorial in his hometown Dallas Dispatch called Bowie "an embarrassing spectacle who should be shelved for his own safety,"

Bowie didn't mind. When a liberal columnist from New York mocked him for being "without doubt, the most venal and remarkably ignorant congressman in history, and that is saying a lot given the sorry composition of that body throughout its history," Bowie took the attack in stride. He sent out a fund-raising message to tell his supporters "they" were once again targeting him and he needed money to stop "them" from silencing him. He raised more than $500,000 in three days.

He voted against every budget proposal and against raising the debt ceiling, saying such policies were unconstitutional and immoral. Bowie joined fellow RAP insurgents in advocating a strategy that bad news about a weakening economy was actually good news. In mid-2015, he welcomed reports that the economy had contracted for a seventh straight quarter and the unemployment rate had reached 17.9 percent.

"The RAP and principled Republicans have worked hard to wreck this wicked economy. This recession is working and shows our austerity agenda to starve and kill government and create a real economy based on the Galtian Imperatives is on track. We don't want some phony economy pumped up on artificial government spending," he told an RAP rally in Washington, D.C., at the Lincoln Memorial. The rally was in support of ratification of a RAP-sponsored constitutional amendment that would make the Galtian Imperatives the only approved economic system in the country.

Like many devoted supporters, Bowie didn't know what the Galtian Imperatives were or what they might do or even if they made economic sense. Those minor details didn't matter. The Galtian Imperatives were biblical in their essence and transcendent in purpose, so practicality was less important than fidelity. Bowie had become a top cheerleader for what the samestream media called the "Galtian Awakening" and he was applauded for supporting a great spiritual force. Bowie was good at preaching, and his sermon at the RAP rally called for lost economic souls to embrace the Galtian Imperatives as "the one and only path to create prosperity for all" and remake the country.

"My fellow patriots, it is vital that we continue to create more tax loopholes for our Guardians of Galt who create wealth and prosperity. Look behind at the statue and words of this great man. Lincoln would have embraced the Galtian Imperatives because he knew we must reward and incentivize our Guardians of Galt. Lincoln understood the importance of boosting the morale of millionaires and billionaires who have been targeted too long for scorn by liberal moochers in the media. Otherwise, we stand to lose our job-creating genius class. No one's tax money should be stolen and wasted on government wickedness, on treacherous programs to serve moochers and takers. The Galtian Imperatives call on us to eliminate these satanic programs at every opportunity. The Galtian Imperatives tell us that government serves us best by not existing at all. The Galtian Imperatives should be enshrined in our constitution," he said to the cheering rally while standing below a large banner that read "Long Live the Galtian Imperatives!"

The so-called truth

Bowie had no shortage of enemies and critics who dismissed him as a fool and court jester, but Bowie was immensely popular to a growing segment of the electorate who appreciated his talents for invention, rampant hyperbole and unapologetic corruption as part of a higher, moneymaking calling. He made a name for himself in Texas and in Real America by dismissing scientific knowledge as "politically biased and un-Real American," calling for the elimination of the idea of government, and admonishing the "moochers among us" for setting a bad influence that threatened all good Texans and Real Americans. He said the moochers should follow his lead

"You see, my friends, Mama Bowie told me I wouldn't learn the right way, the Real American way, in some Ivy League finishing school," Bowie said in one of his stock campaign speeches. "My lessons come from the land, from the tough choices I had to make to realize my genius."

Bowie told his biography often and with many variations of climbing from the depths of poverty, a native Texan from the hill country raised by a blind single mother. He became a teenage preacher and a snake-charming healer who had climbed the ladder of success without the help of sinful "government slavery" programs, he liked to say. Bowie believed that all Real Americans should follow his lead on the Real American stairway to success. "We must go backward and eliminate completely the virus of liberal do-goodism which weakens us morally and economically. We must destroy the liberal history and its New Deal pandering to the moochers and the so-called middle class. When we eliminate the past, we can march forward and bravely into a golden age foretold by the Galtian Imperatives," Bowie said.

While inspiring, the essential elements of his personal tale were fabricated, as reporters discovered without too much investigative effort. Bowie wasn't much of a teenage preacher though he did have a mail-order divinity degree and he handled a garter snake once. His doting mother, Sarah, wore thick glasses but wasn't blind, and they were federal witness protection program transplants from Philadelphia who had been given new identifications. Anthony Regalo became Lawrence Charles Bowie and grew up in a modest, lower middle-class home in Austin. Mother and son were assisted by programs such as Social Security Disability Insurance, Head Start, food stamps, Medicaid and student loans for Bowie's college education. Sarah herself finished her college studies and became an elementary school teacher.

When reporters talked to Sarah Bowie, they discovered she was a liberal-leaning voter and while she didn't agree with her son politically, she was puzzled by her his habit of merging incoherence with untruths. "Who are you talking about, Lawrence?" Sarah would say to him when he talked about their struggle upward as part of a typical campaign speech. "I was never blind. We got assistance, not a lot of it, but it did help keep us sheltered and fed and you were schooled and I went to school. So what you're saying isn't much true."

"Mama, don't you worry about the so-called truth. All that matters is that people believe," Bowie said to his mother after one campaign speech in which he vilified the "hordes of takers" who were bankrupting Real America financially and spiritually. Like any good mother, she had a blind spot when it came to her son. She may have protested, but that was Mama Bowie simply being Mama Bowie, sometimes literal to a fault when it came to notions of telling the truth and attempting to accommodate reality.

As his legacy showed again and again, her son had no such qualms about the truth and didn't care much for reality. He knew what was vital and what mattered most to him was that facts were irrelevant unless they could serve his evolving self-interest. In his best-selling 2016 campaign autobiography *The Audacity of My Liberty*, Bowie said his character was built on the pillars of self-reliance, making money, honestly reported corruption, unregulated liberty, incoherence, traditional family values (that made allowances for one current wife, two ex-wives, six children with two born out of wedlock, and two mistresses), and an unquestioned devotion to the Galtian Imperatives. He promised under no circumstances would he ever be "troubled or bothered by fact checkers who deviously rearrange the truth for their own gain and contribute nothing to society but anxiety and doubt" about the glorious Galtian epoch to come.

"Do facts matter? Of course they don't, especially when they contain seeds of moocher political agendas. Facts are for girly-men and do-gooders who care about such trivial distinctions," said Bowie, quoting from his book during a speech to the congregation of the Holy Grail Church of Redemption, Resurrection and Revival in Dallas. "Real men, Real Americans ignore the facts and pay homage to their gut instincts, which they know are right. I don't believe in history, I don't believe there is a real history that the liberal cowards and moocher takers would have you believe. There is no history, only the glory of Real American faith."

Bowie was considered a trailblazer for combining prayer events and political speeches at venues such as the Holy Grail Church of Redemption, Resurrection and Revival. The church became his favorite photo-op prop before or after major policy announcements, in part because Bowie thought it proper to "finally obliterate that cruel liberal separation of church and state. They should be one and the same."

All hail Bowie

As his reputation grew, Bowie received more attention as "a serious, possibly determining force in American politics," wrote Tom Yossairan, a popular and pioneering RAP repblogger who became one of Bowie's biggest advocates. "The incoherent genius of Bowieism is a new and awe-inspiring phenomenon that can't be ignored by the moocher hordes."

Bowie was a big man of ever-broadening girth, seemingly taller than his actual height due to the lift from high-heeled custom-made cowboy boots adorned with "Mama Bowie" on each boot. He had a blonde hair buzz cut on a head that looked too small to be sitting on his shoulders. He often deployed a wry smile that invited speculation of all kinds and his friends and enemies were amazed at his talent for taking a mediocre political poker hand and daring people to call his bluff. Despite his ferocious rhetoric, those close to Bowie said he was man of good humor and loyalty to those who served him.

Bowie was especially adept at preaching the gospel of Randian free market magic even though his own business career was hardly inspiring and he found reading the prophet Ayn Rand difficult (he hired for his Congressional office a Rand disciple who provided daily Galtian perspective summaries on current events). A star linebacker at Middle Texas State, he liked to point out that he turned down a professional football career to serve a greater cause. Though it was true that he played with immense grit and determination, it was bad knees and tortoise-slow speed that ensured he would need to pursue other opportunities – but, as he liked to tell his supporters, it made for a quality character-enhancing line and that's really all that mattered.

Bowie went through occupations in a hurry. By the age of 35, Bowie was the manager of a five-lot used car franchise in Fort Worth when he finally got his big break. A former employer and Republican Party official remembered Bowie's tenacity, if not his talent, and recommended Bowie for a job as a political collection man. Until that point in his life, Bowie hadn't paid much attention to politics, but this was an opportunity and a revelation. He told an aide later, "My talent for shaking down corporate moneymen came as naturally as breathing."

Once he found his path, Bowie rose quickly and ruthlessly (he never lost an election) and he made an important discovery in 2002 during his first run as a candidate for the Texas state senate – the more he lied, the more he stretched the truth beyond recognition, the less people cared.

He noticed that his supporters in particular and most voters overall had bad memories. When economic and political conditions worsened, their memories disappeared altogether. "The taller the tale, the easier the sale," he proudly told a reporter.

Later as governor, Bowie claimed the economic miracle in the Real American Republic of Texas, also known as RART, set a high standard for other states to follow. "Yes, we are proud of our 26 percent unemployment rate and that we cut business taxes and labor costs again and again," Bowie had said at the spring 2017 meeting of the Real American Party Governor's Association. "We invite businesses large and small to move here and experience the Texas miracle of almost slave labor wages. We have privatized every vital state function. Hell, we've even privatized the privatization office and I've taken steps to privatize myself." The applause from his political peers was thunderous and there was increasing talk in RAP pundit circles that Bowie had presidential credibility as the country fell into another period of deep recession and negative economic growth.

"Real America needs a strong, bold and visionary leader who understands that the pill of cleansing austerity must be swallowed to save the nation from liberal fantasies of good government. Through his innovations, Bowie continues to set the standard for defeating weak-kneed appeasers who believe taxing the rich and talented is sound policy," said Betty Gagun, an influential columnist for the Galt Street Journal, after Bowie had sold the toll rights for all federal interstate highways to corporate friends and supporters. When Bowie seized the highways there was media speculation that the federal government would fight back. But he was helped by the 2016 elections that thrust the RAP into power and the historical RAP congressional coup of early 2017. Bowie calculated correctly that the feds had no stomach or financial will to fight back. And he made a hefty finder's fee for his political bravado.

Are you RA?

Before becoming governor, Bowie served in Congress as a reliable Mad Hatter Republican in a Dallas suburban district so safe that, it was said by political commentators, the incumbent couldn't lose unless he died or was found alive in bed naked with at least two men. It was both scenarios that did in Bowie's predecessor who died after being found alive in bed naked with three men. Bowie arrived in Washington via the historic Mad Hatter wave election of 2010 and he wasted no time in unveiling his legislative style of simmering, evangelical outrage. In addition to becoming the leader of the Imbecile Caucus, he proudly advertised the fact that he hadn't come to Washington to do anything except to "blow this place up, destroy every vestige of government and join my fellow patriots in pissing on the remains."

Bowie chose his advisors wisely. Chip Howlen, Bowie's chief-of-staff and trusted legislative aide, had been the top pesticide salesman in San Antonio. Bowie had been impressed when he read that Howlen had been indicted three times and imprisoned once for defying federal environmental regulations about dumping poison in municipal water supplies. "You have to admire a man who stands up for what he believes," Bowie said at Howlen's parole hearing. "He said it was more economically efficient and profitable for him to dump those chemicals and by God, he did it. We should admire men of this creed and give them awards, not put them in prison."

Howlen became the perfect aide for Bowie. He proudly and publicly declared he knew nothing about legislative processes or even the purpose of congressional committees. "It's all a waste of time and a shameful abuse of taxpayer's money," Howlen said in response to a question why Bowie rarely attended hearings of his assigned committees during his time in Congress. "People didn't send us here to get smarter. They sent us here to cut taxes and shit on government at every opportunity. They want us to make sure that nothing gets done."

Howlen also made news by telling constituents who asked for help in matters such as veterans' health care or Social Security benefits to "not bother us with your whining. People need to straighten up and not expect anything from us or the government." Howlen also promised to "kick the ass" of reporters who dared to criticize Bowie. Not surprisingly, when Howlen walked the corridors of the House office building, reporters scattered out of his way.

Quite unintentionally, Bowie had created a circus atmosphere that attracted a colorful cast of characters who were devoted to him, including one man who set up a station outside of Bowie's district office and guarded it with an assault rifle and two semi-automatic pistols. "I'm gonna shoot anyone who comes here to cause trouble and threaten Congressman Bowie's reputation and his mission from God," said Ted Vickers, a former insane asylum inmate. Vickers found his new home after he was released due to state budget cuts in Texas. Bowie's predecessor as governor had abolished mental illness and therefore the state was free from any further obligations. Vicker's later briefly served as the chief of Gov. Bowie's security detail before he resigned to lead a militia battalion in Louisissippi.

Bowie took advantage of the disintegrating political environment to mature into a shrewd tactician. "The people out there think it is all one bad reality TV show and who can blame them? So I figure it's not my job to tell 'em any different. I don't worry about their bad memories or bother educating them. Let's just serve up healthy doses of manufactured crises and hysteria along a heaping supply of scapegoats," Bowie said during an editorial board meeting with the conservative repblog site Liberal Hating Daily.

By the end of his second term in 2014, Bowie hit his rhetorical stride. He gained national attention for railing on the House floor against the "entrenched class" of liberal traitors and Republican appeasers. "I was sent to Congress to do nothing and for four years I have done nothing but fight the demon seed of liberalism and smite the moocher enemies of John Galt," Bowie said in one memorable floor speech that gave him his nickname and was replayed over 2 million times on RAPTube. "We must protect our exalted Guardians of Galt by any and all hysteric measures. We should begin to outlaw liberals and collectivist thinking and not hesitate to break up this temple and stop its evil spending ways. It's time to shut the country down. We need to restore the gold standard and baptize Real America with obedience to liberty and the Galtian Imperatives."

As was often noted by political commentators, Bowie had an uncanny sense of political timing. The 2012 re-election of Democratic President Burt Octavian was the final betrayal to the new breed of uncompromising patriots like Bowie. The patriots blamed the country, and especially the Republican Party, for a lack of backbone in not preventing the re-election of an African-American president and that made their blood boil. They considered Octavian a danger to liberty and freedom and their gun collections. He was a socialist, communist, a black nationalist, anti-colonial racist and fascist hater of the free market system. Octavian also was a constitutional usurper who should be impeached and removed from office because it was proven he was born in Africa and Indonesia simultaneously.

Bowie did not make it easy for those who yearned for a more cooperative working environment. Each time Octavian made an attempt to forge
a bipartisan consensus on the proper naming of post offices, Bowie and
his fellow patriots distrusted him even more and accused him of satanic
machinations and hating white people.

"We blame this imposter president for our incoherence because like
Satan, he has multiple disguises. It's not our fault we don't know who
he is or how he hides behind his treachery," Bowie told the Greater
Dallas Mad Hatter Club. Many noted that Bowie appeared to take his
anti-Octavian cause to an obsessive level. He had been outraged in 2008
when Octavian was elected to his first term. "I told my Mama Bowie
that this evil creature from the dark underground pits of hell forced me
to run for Congress because we needed to fight back and take a stand,
maybe a last stand, to get our country back," Bowie said during the first
campaign for Congress in 2010. He neglected to add that Mama Bowie
voted for Octavian. When Octavian was re-elected, it was too much
for Bowie who urged his fellow Mad Hatter Republicans to pass a bill
declaring a national state of mourning until Octavian's term of office
ended in January 2017.

And then came the historical moment which seized the imaginations of
anti-Octavian patriots across the country. Bowie and his fellow patriots
had not gotten over the 2012 election and he told a crowd of agitated
patriots in early 2014 that there must have been treason at the highest
levels for this "abomination of democracy to happen." Bowie said. Prior
to the 2012 election, numerous Republican-controlled states had passed
legislation to make voting more difficult for non-Republicans, but the
initiatives didn't stop people from voting and supporting Octavian.

"What kind of fools were we? We passed laws designed to disenfran-
chise moocher voters and then we lose the election. This wasn't rocket

science. It was just a matter of will power to stop the parasites from voting. These moochers were spell bound and easily bribed with gifts from
this satanic president," Bowie shouted at the 323rd Impeach Octavian
Now rally since the 2012 election. "The majority looters and moochers do not deserve the right to rule. Real Americans know what I am
talking about. Real Americans should not let this wicked practice of
majority rule happen ever again." The response was thunderous and ac-
companied with repeated shouts of "Kill the moochers!" and "Hang the
takers!" and "We are the Real Americans!"

Thus the history-altering movement was born and the terms Real
America, Real Americans and Real Americanism were catapulted into
political prominence. Within days, "Are you RA?" became the new shib-
boleth for the true believers of a Real America.

Mama Bowie knows best

Never one to bypass an opportunity to serve his ambition while proving
his bona fides as a money maker, Bowie became the public face behind
the new patriot rebranding transformation to the Real American Party.
By the middle of 2014, the RAP began severing bonds with Washington
insiders as an increasing number of influential corporate donors began
to support the RAP faction. In return for their financial support, Bowie
promised to "put on a show."

Bowie became an RAP folk hero by making it a point to never say
Octavian's name or even acknowledge that he was actually president.
He became one of the most vocal congressional leaders of the resistance
against Octavian and he made alliances with the compliant Washington,
D.C. samestream media complex that regarded him as a colorful example of the "principled" opposition. He became a sought-after presence
by producers of political talk shows who were unconcerned about his

incoherence but loved the hometown references to "Mama Bowie" that he often sprinkled into his messaging rants.

"We have been victimized yet again. Mama Bowie said we should never compromise with this illegitimate president who is a Black Muslim plant that suckled at the breasts of terrorists and has resurrected the Black Panther Party to kill law-abiding white patriots. He is an odious pretender and his America-hating minions must be stopped," Bowie said at the first Real America Political Action Committee meeting in April 2014. "We are the resistance, the last line of defense against this tyranny. There can be no compromise, no quarter. The looters, moochers and takers represent the most dastardly evil front that this country has ever faced."

When the Secret Service asked Bowie to tone down rhetoric that had unleashed a flood of death threats against the president, Bowie called a press conference and denounced those "who would silence Real Americans protesting against the tyranny of this illegitimate regime." Bowie also milked the controversy and sent out his 45th fund raising appeal of the year. This one raised an estimated $3 million for the Real American Party in a week.

Bowie gave a stirring speech on the House floor in support of the 2015 Anti-Equalization of Opportunity law proposed by the Real American Party minority in Congress. The law had no chance of passing but Bowie said it was important to take a principled stand against fictional legislation and he implored "all Real Americans who care about the future" to join him in the fight. "We saw in the pages of our great modern Bible *Atlas Shrugged* how the liberal looters and moochers used a hideous law to destroy the country by draining it of ambition and imposing a collective mind set. We can't let that happen again. Mama Bowie told me we must never be all in this together because it stifles individual genius and reduces opportunities for profitable exploitation," he said.

A government worth hating

Bowie, who falsely but boldly claimed ancestral lineage to one of the mythical heroes at the Alamo in 1836, became a national legend when his single-minded gubernatorial campaign promise to create "a government worth hating" catapulted him to victory in 2016. "I hate government at every level because it's an evil spell designed to take away our God-given liberties," he said at every stop on the campaign trail in Texas and in every television ad. "Are my weak-kneed opponents willing to promise you a government worth hating? I tell you, my fellow Texas patriots, I stand before you and make this solemn promise: if you hate government as much as I do, vote for me and I will give you a Texas state government worth hating."

Texas voters loved the message and Bowie didn't have too many worries once he made it through the RAP primary with Someret. The voting suppression failures from 2012 had become a distant memory by 2016. Though many commentators had said a few years before that due to dramatically shifting voter demographic patterns, Texas would likely change from a liberty and maker state to a moocher and looter socialist paradise, Bowie easily won the election, which saw more than 40 percent of the 2012 electorate disqualified due to stringent birth certificate and income requirements. The new laws eliminated an overwhelming majority of "other than Caucasian" voters, including the majority Hispanic population.

When Ben, his African-American campaign driver, asked Bowie what had happened to his voting rights, Bowie put on arm on Ben's shoulder and comforted him. "Now Ben, this isn't about race or bigotry or none of that nasty name-calling stuff, so don't take it personal. We were victimized time and again until our Texas Liberty Court stepped in and took action. They agreed that this outdated one-man one-vote scheme endangered our rights to exist as a party because there were more of you than of us. If your urban kind had just voted the right way, then we wouldn't be having this conversation."

After two months in the governor's office, his favorability rating dipped below 10 percent, even among members of his RAP base. But Bowie was undeterred and in fact felt vindicated. Unpopularity, after all, was exactly the point and was in fact the new measurement for real popularity. He held a press conference saying he was succeeding in giving liberty-loving people a government worth hating. He added that the trend would continue as he filled the positions in the shrinking state government with "unqualified and incompetent Real American patriots who love liberty and believe that good government is evil government."

Bowie also proudly and publicly pocketed major bribes for being a leading proponent of changing the currency in RAP-led states from dollars to the faith-based Real American Currency that took place in early 2017. "We won the country back in 2016 and we should not hesitate to protect the future by creating a currency that reflects our Real American values," Bowie testified at a Congressional hearing. "I am proud to be paid a referral fee from speculators for my hard work."

If the good patriots of RART expected a do-nothing governor when Bowie was elected, they were wrong as he moved quickly and with great velocity. He had read his Galt (or at least had Galt read to him by a new Galtian seer he added to his statehouse staff) and knew the times demanded decisive action by men of genius. Within days of taking office, he maneuvered an RAP lawmaker to insert fine print into a bill giving him emergency executive authority to do "what is necessary to protect the Galtian Imperatives and to uphold the dignity and honor of the Real American Party."

Reporters discovered the new powers law by accident when it was inserted as an amendment in a new law that, after extensive review by a RAP panel of experts, ordered high school history textbooks in Texas to conclude that the South had indeed won the Civil War. The new textbook measure also declared that the Ku Klux Klan was the first and greatest civil rights organization in the country's history. The textbook authors were also ordered to compliment slaveholders for being "trailblazers for the Galtian Imperatives." The slave masters were to be "positively cited" for providing room, board and vocational opportunities to their grateful slaves.

Bowie justified his stealth approach by assuring supporters that "the logic is sound. The fact that we needed emergency powers and asked for them secretly proves that there is a secret emergency requiring these powers."

Bowie thus became the law in the Real American Republic of Texas and had unknowingly paved the way for The Execution Channel.

CHAPTER TWO

347

"There's no use trying," Alice said. "One can't believe impossible things."
"I daresay you haven't had much practice," said the White Queen.
"When I was your age, I always did it for half-an-hour a day.
Why, sometimes I've believed as many as six impossible things
before breakfast."

– LEWIS CARROLL, THROUGH THE LOOKING GLASS

G ov. Bowie would later promote himself as the sledgehammer that smashed through regulatory and political barriers to make the Execution Channel a reality but, and this may come as a shock to many who know no other version, Jason Bravtart was the idea man. He was the visionary who gave it life and crafted its shape and scope. And as with many great ideas, it was born out of desperation.

For most of his adult life, Bravtart's daily mantra had been "There but for the grace of Galt, go I." He told his wife, Sandy, and friends this was homage to the unalterable fact that he was destined for greatness and was halfway up the pinnacle of success at the age of 32. "I have always been a Real American and was one even before great patriots imagined and then began to create a Real America," he once said to a political columnist who had pronounced Jason the first "great propagandist of the 21st century."

Bravtart was certain he was guided by a special force. He was known for embracing his genius without apology and was fearless in playing the victimization card. "The genius class has been victimized for far too long. Why do the majority moochers always complain about injustice and create laws that emasculate job creators and money-making geniuses? They do it because they are cowards who need government to provide them with meaning," he said in an interview with L.A. Militia Times in 2017.

By the time reality television show producer Bravtart came up with the history-changing idea of the Execution Channel in mid-2017, he had spent a year in professional exile. This time adrift had not been kind to him and it seemed more like a century. It was a sad state of affairs he considered an abomination and forced upon him, he told his wife, by a conspiracy of "looters, cowards and bandits." It had been a dizzying fall from grace for the former wonder boy of conservative alternative media who had parlayed his talent as a video political hit man for hire into national acclaim – and a $23.5 million Hollywood Hills home – but his daily mantra reminded him that no matter the long odds, his genius best was yet to come.

Despite a fall from grace, which we will consider shortly in greater detail, he had good reason to hope for redemption. Bravtart had gained international fame as the creator of the political reality television show megahit *Foreclosure Justice*. It was a groundbreaking show that chronicled the heroic efforts of bankers, debt collectors, judges, bounty hunters, prosecutors, process servers and law enforcement officials to evict ungrateful takers and moochers who had stopped paying their mortgages following the second great housing industry collapse in 2014.

Bravtart calculated correctly that audiences would embrace the formula and he made a fortune because viewers couldn't get enough of the reality procedural. He had choreographed a morality play that included sheriffs or judges (who liked getting some camera time) reading writs of legal eviction in dramatic language. Viewers applauded when families were tossed out of their former homes, often without warning, for dramatic effect. The final segment of each episode captured families shamed by an on-the-ground correspondent who insisted they take personal responsibility for their lives and confess their role as moochers undermining the country's economy. It didn't matter that a few times the being evicted had in fact kept up with their payments and were shocked by what was happening.

What mattered, Jason often said, is that each week the public and national humiliation of two to three families provided moral substance and measured doses of righteous indignation for the audience. "We must celebrate those who defend the Galtian Imperatives and highlight the consequences of justice for those parasites who have earned their infamy," Bravtart said when he received the Joe McCarthy Real American Media Courage award in 2016. *Foreclosure Justice* launched a wave of Real American justice reality show copycats and a new genre called RealAmerPolTV. *Foreclosure Justice* led the pack with exceptionally high ratings and was a favorite for advertisers seeking that crucial 45- to 54-year-old, 0.25 percent wealth demographic.

But a year after he sold his stake in *Foreclosure Justice* to a consortium of Baltic hedge fund managers, Bravtart couldn't halt a career slide he believed was in perilous descent. His legacy as a conservative media pioneer no longer mattered. He had been a 'take no prisoner' young Republican turned passionate Mad Hatter Party booster and then an enthusiastic supporter of the Real American Party in its early days. But such credentials seemed to have no relevance as he pondered his future while Real America was being reshaped and redefined with each passing day. He fought feeling sorry for himself but sometimes it was a losing battle.

"I was the one who created the public image of the Real America Party, from the new flag with the distinctive RA logo to the 'I am a maker not a moocher' signs that hang in the windows of a million businesses across the country," he said to a reporter from the Galt Street Journal who was researching an article about Bravtart's rise and fall. "I helped define the RAP, set them apart as a historical game-changing force for good. No organization had better propaganda starting out than the RAP. Now I am damaged goods reduced to producing militia marketing videos. This was not part of my plan. My genius deserves better."

Reality be damned

He had planned a much different future only a year earlier. Bravtart felt certain of a huge and profitable success for his immediate follow-up creation, *The Real Homeless of Malibu Beach*. It was, friendly reviewers said, a Jason Bravtart specialty. He captured the day-to-day activities of homeless people cashing unemployment and Social Security checks, trading food stamps for shelter and medical marijuana, using their government-supplied mobile phones to order Chinese food deliveries and partaking in comfortable cardboard housing. Some of the homeless talked of "being owed" benefits for being homeless and they shared philosophical observations about homelessness as a "brave lifestyle choice" that deserved respect, appreciation and financial support from the public.

Bravtart said the show proved to the country that the homeless were not down on their luck, that their misfortune was a myth invented by the "looter liberal mob" to waste taxpayer money and distract attention from vital issues such as more tax cuts and subsidies for the Guardians of Galt. Bravtart aimed to prove yet again that assistance for the so-called poor represented a government subsidized bribe for votes of the moocher class and some of the homeless on the show did talk about selling their votes to politicians who gave them the "most gifts." The homeless also rejected the Galtian Imperatives for being harsh on the poor. The "samestream media" had abetted in the creation of a lie designed to give moral stature to moochers who didn't deserve it, Bravtart told advertisers who were eagerly lining up to sponsor the show.

After a strong two-episode start that drew even bigger ratings than at the same juncture for *Foreclosure Justice*, the show ran aground abruptly. Bravrtart was blindsided by confidential sources that had tipped off hundreds of repbloggers across the country with a show-stopping revelation. The characters in *The Real Homeless* were not the real homeless but paid actors reading from Bravtart's scripts. Bravtart, the master of spin, could not control the story and it quickly evolved into a national media firestorm.

At first Bravtart stood tall and issued a non-denial denial through his public relations firm. When that did not satisfy his backers or his critics, he issued another statement, a combative response saying that the show "captured an essential truth of those who undermine the vitality of our Randian economic system and who violate our sacred Galtian Imperatives. Does it really matter if the characters are paid actors if the moochers and looters they portray are real? We act on our convictions and say that reality is what we say it is and that we portray an essential truth that is more relevant than imposed facts and liberal notions of reality. We challenge our critics to dispute not only the premise of our weekly expose into the heart of this parasitic subculture but the corrupt political ideology that sustains it. What are their priorities?"

His counterattack gained no momentum. Even constructive critics said Bravtart had pushed the straw man argument too far, considering that investigative bloggers found there were no actual homeless in Malibu Beach. No one in Malibu Beach, investigative bloggers reported, collected unemployment checks or food stamps which had been eliminated due to federal government cutbacks. The influential Galt Street Journal, a strong supporter of *Foreclosure Justice*, had hailed the arrival of *The Real Homeless of Malibu Beach* and said in an editorial the homeless were a "parasitic danger that threatens the moral fiber of all Real Americans." But the editorial pointed out the real homeless in that region had been rounded up and sent away to other municipalities, a fact that Bravtart would have known had he "done even a touch of real research." The editorial also cast doubt on his methods. "If Bravtart wants to expand his viewership and gain greater political sympathy, he should at least acknowledge a small dose of reality," the editorial said.

Bravtart was devastated by the Galt Street Journal rebuke, which he considered a dagger to his heart. "Since when did reality matter?" he screamed on the phone at a Galt Street Journal junior editorial page editor who agreed with him but could do little else. Mild though it was, Bravtart understood immediately this national slap down by the Galt Street Journal could be a career killer. The resulting ideological fire-fight over the nature of political reality lasted for months and took place against the backdrop of the birth of Real America. It also took center stage on political talk radio and televinet shows and even briefly eclipsed popular conspiracy reports of liberal traitors attempting to secretly impose Islamic Sharia Law in 2014.

The debate did not help Bravtart who lost more than $5 million of his own money. He had put his show on the commodity futures market and bet heavily on its success. Production was halted suddenly when a core of once avid advertisers dropped their support. "We choose at this time to reconsider our advertising options," said a spokesman for Ensonic Energy.

Ensonic had planned to use its support for *The Real Homeless* as a propaganda platform to rehabilitate its image as a benevolent job-creating corporation with millions of "honest, hard-working investors." The rehabilitation was considered necessary after investigators said the company had retroactively raised electric prices by 235 percent and shut off electricity to millions of people who couldn't pay their bills in the middle of a heat wave in 2015. More than 645 people died and the CEO complained about the backlash. "If we are not going to exploit people at their most vulnerable, what's the point?" he said at Congressional hearing. Ensonic eventually paid a $500,000 fine and was congratulated by government officials for stepping up and doing the right thing for its own good. In return, Congress passed a law giving the company full immunity for its actions.

Bravtart knew that if Ensonic was concerned about bad public relations other companies would follow suit and they did. Then his South American investor group pulled support and demanded its money back and another $7 million was lost. When a Los Angeles Journal entertainment reporter asked him why the show had been canceled by the Reality Now Network, Bravtart responded in the manner of a once bulletproof character stunned by a plot twist. "My highest virtue is to make money, a lot of it. I know the game and accept that advertisers remain the ultimate arbiter, as they should be. They didn't like the political sideshow discussions about the finer points of reality. I guess the faking poor can't compete with the real dying," he said in reference to the most popular show at the time *Celebrity Life or Death Survival: Mojave Desert.*

Publicly, he put on a brave face, but privately he felt devastated. It didn't help when a reporter contacted his politically estranged father, who didn't mind seeing his son brought down. "It serves him right. Maybe this will teach him some humility and he will learn lessons about the perils of dabbling in the voodoo of alternative reality," said Congressman Jack Bravtart, a Democrat from New Hampshire.

Jason felt no humility, no remorse. He felt victimized and resentful of his fate. He considered *The Real Homeless of Malibu Beach* to be a master stroke of political and cultural timing to coincide with budding legislative efforts in Real American states such as Texas to have the privileged poor pay more taxes, to have more "skin in the game." That he had used actors to highlight this essential point was less concerning to him than a greater doubt that he had lost the touch of understanding public taste.

During his glory days of *Foreclosure Justice,* he considered his connection to the American viewing public almost spiritual. "My genius, as I understand it, is that I can sense that the American people yearn for the type of collective experience they had with television in the 1950s and 1960s," he said in a New York Journal profile in 2015. "*Foreclosure Justice* is the 21st century version of *Gunsmoke.* The archetypes and myths about real justice and reinforcing the strengths of a proper way of life are as important today as they were then."

Jason wondered who had tipped off "the media vultures that destroyed me" and came to one conclusion – the moochers and looters had ambushed him and undermined the genius of *The Real Homeless of Malibu Beach.* He didn't know if it had been fellow Real Americans or subversive liberal traitors hidden in Real American cloaks but it didn't matter. "Those looters hate my talent and vision and could do no better than stop me from making money and telling the truth," Bravtart told his publicist and former mistress Cassie Blight. Cassie agreed with him, of course, but also thought that he might have gone too far when he elevated his setback to the equivalent of natural disaster like the fall of Atlantis. "Not sure I see the grave existential crisis or societal collapse here, but Jason can be very dramatic about some matters," Cassie told her psychic, Penelope.

Searching for meaning

The private despair Bravtart felt led to an endless series of anxiety attacks, often during the night. He feared that a new generation of activists and producers, even more cutthroat and sensationalist than he had ᴜᴄᴄɴ, would emerge to dominate the industry. During the final stretch of his exile, Bravtart awoke night after night with a pounding heart at the same time, 3:47 a.m.

He awoke as if on cue at 3:47 a.m. and every morning he put on his running shorts and a *Foreclosure Justice* T-shirt in preparation for his morning 10-mile run on and around Mulholland Drive. Even during his heyday, he had worked out faithfully, but being on the sideline turned him into a workout fanatic. He began to compete and place well for an amateur in grueling quadathlon events – a two-mile military obstacle course under live machine gun and rocket propelled grenade fire was a recent addition to the triathlon mix – but the extra physical activity seemed to have little impact.

Bravtart was agnostic when it came to superstitions but he became a closet numerologist who found comfort and mystery in numbers. He tried to decipher the code of 347, of why he was waking up at that precise time. He was looking for meaning in 347 as he jumped out of bed while his wife Sandy slept soundly. He knew seven was critical, the number that represented spiritual power in the universe, and in this case it meant Galtian energy driving all things. He sensed that three, which represented the third dimension, and four, which reflected the illusion of time and solidity, adding to seven was his likely path to redemption.

There were days when he felt his lean 6-foot frame beginning to recede, along with his closely cut hairline. It hurt him that his phone calls and e-messages went unreturned from former colleagues, many of whom he had mentored in the fundamentals in this new age of political assassination and provocative propaganda. Having a series or two canceled was one thing. Hell, he told himself, even the best football coaches were fired. But Jason thought that to become persona non grata in an industry he had helped invent and take to its fullest potential was a hideous outcome. There was an evil envy in those who had sidelined him, like those who had mocked the great John Galt Line of railroad progress. How could he show them they were wrong, that his genius was so righteous and obvious?

It was a profound question that haunted his wife, Sandra. They had met during production of the first episode of *Foreclosure Justice* when she had been featured as a heroic bank officer who wore a pistol and confronted the challenges of getting moochers out of foreclosed houses, especially those who fought the process and claimed they had been current with their payments. "We believe there will be a time when you become moochers and better for us to perform the surgery now," Sandy said in a famous heated exchange with a lawyer in Episode 3 of the show. They had fallen in love quickly and with great passion, a romance heightened by her discovery of the Randian universe and John Galt. As their love blossomed, they would read out loud entire chapters of *Atlas Shrugged* and *The Fountainhead* to each other in bed before and after lovemaking. She told her parents she was proud that Jason had a "true genius at knowing the lowest depth of public taste."

But two years into a wonderful marriage of kindred spirits, Sandy told her psychic Penelope (the same Penelope who counseled Cassie Blight) that she was concerned Jason might slide down the long slope of pity and self-doubt. "I've encouraged him to keep busy, to lecture wayward souls at the neighborhood Galt Reclamation Camp or add vintage Vietnam-era M-16s or AK-15s to his gun collection," Sandy said to Penelope, the psychic who had envisioned a life-altering love affair for Sandy days before she met Jason. Sandy considered Penelope a true seer. She hoped that Penelope could see a path forward for Jason.

When Jason thought he was at his lowest point, Sandy returned from one of her thrice-weekly visits with Penelope and shared the good news with Jason. "Penelope has seen the first stages of your comeback and it will be glorious." She didn't dare tell him that she hoped the return to glory was real and would result more in substantial payoffs than fame.

Sandy worked as the chief marketing officer for the 1st John Galt SoCal Militia and her star was on the rise. She had gained a reputation nationally for her militia marketing work and for expanding militia influence into the forced protection and financial services sectors. Sandy was also branching out into the music industry and had become manager of The Liberators, a punk/Goth/metal militia band who developed a strong following in Real America with the hit "Kissing the USA Goodbye."

Sandy was concerned about how quickly their RAC and foreign assets were dwindling. Just over the past year, she had watched their savings drop to 7,800,000 RAC. Though their income and capital gains tax burden had mostly vanished after the Save Real America Now tax reforms of 2017 and the change to RAC, she was worried about the long-term prospects for keeping up their standard of living.

As with many in the top maker economic class, security from moochers and looters was becoming ever more expensive by the day. Sandy figured it was costing some 2 million RAC annually just to maintain and upgrade their technological and human security protection and for forensic accountant specialists to protect their wealth. Running the gauntlet of spontaneous flash mobs of anti-Real America protestors, roaming gangs of ethnic marauders, and real thieves and kidnappers just to get home was becoming a chore. It had to be done more and more with a two-convoy security detail of six mercenaries. Though Sandy had managed to give Jason some work producing militia recruiting videos and televinet commercials, she was concerned they could keep up their standard of living only for the next five to seven years unless Jason started to make significant money again.

Sandy was the same height as Jason and had played college basketball. She had red hair and strikingly pale skin adorned with freckles. Jason teased her that when she smiled or got excited her freckles got brighter. That was often the case when she returned from her visits with Penelope the Psychic. Jason often winced when she returned from her Penelope sessions. He admired the con that Penelope ran – not only was she a fake psychic but likely a closet liberal or politically agnostic, which in itself was subversive. At times he was annoyed that she was taking RAC from Real American citizens but he never moved to turn her in to the local RAP militia. Sandra was smitten by Penelope's con and Jason did nothing to discourage her enthusiasm. And besides, he figured, if Penelope was a true security threat, Sandy was vested with militia arresting power and could grab Penelope at any time if she wanted.

One day Sandy returned from a session with shining freckles. "Penelope is certain of a comeback, just not when. She sees clearly that your comeback will not just make headlines and restore you to your rightful place, but it will change the course of Real American history," Sandra said.

On this point, Jason wanted to believe. Like anyone down on his luck, he wanted a comeback, but the exile had heightened his ambitions and resentment. He was terrified he might get sucked down further and become part of the moocher class. He already felt he was becoming a moocher to Sandy. Every morning he woke up at 3:47, he burned for a return to glory worthy of a Randian hero. He wanted to reclaim his rightful place as a major money maker and thought leader.

As his resentment increased, his ambitions soared. A hit show wasn't enough. Though the golden age for fictional industrial geniuses such as John Galt had passed, a new generation of financial and digital makers had forged a new frontier of exposing moocher and looter public consensus through fear and market-driven propaganda. Jason wanted to be a great maker again and a taker down of moochers and looters. He needed a larger platform, a chance to become a titan of industry and influence, his face again on the cover of the Galt Street Journal. Imagine Galt and you can make it happen was the other mantra he told himself three times daily. Jason sometimes repeated his destiny-altering prayer in anger, sometimes in desperation, but always with the conviction that he would triumph in the end like John Galt. Jason knew something big what going to happen.

A lifeline found

As Jason puzzled for weeks over the cosmic meaning of 347, his road to redemption began to fall into place, albeit slowly. During this exile, Jason discovered he had an important fan and that contact that would prove pivotal when his Execution Channel vision came into focus. At a Real American Party political fundraiser in Hollywood, Jason was attempting to revitalize his networking prowess. He was talking to a militia colonel from Arizona when a well-dressed but strange looking man of dwarf-like height materialized by Bravtart's side with a mobile phone. When Jason looked down, the man's expressionless face did not change as he handed the phone to Jason. "Chairman Frimmer requires your attention, Mr. Bravtart," said the messenger with a soothing metronomic voice.

Jason's eyes widened. James "Big Stake" Frimmer was a no-nonsense billionaire speculator who had proven his mettle time and again. Frimmer, whose mere existence was debated heavily throughout the country, had enhanced his fortune by selling bad mortgages to unsuspecting investors a decade before. Frimmer then became a national icon when he made even more money by creating and then selling the nation's largest foreclosure services operation – in fact, Jason mined contacts in Frimmer's various companies for top-notch story leads in *Foreclosure Justice*. Jason admired Frimmer's courageous innovation, which proved that capitalism freed from the bonds of regulatory chains and government meddling worked as perfectly as the Galtian Imperatives had prophesized. It was rumored that Frimmer had thousands of politicians, officials, and other useful types on his vast payroll, but rumors far outnumbered hard facts about Frimmer and his vast operation. It was presumed he was all powerful and omnipresent like the sun. Jason was honored that Frimmer even knew who he was.

Jason stood at attention and said "Greetings, Patriot" into the phone.

"I like you Bravtart and I don't why those network peons canceled that homeless show of yours last year. That was sheer genius." Frimmer, who didn't bother with what he considered the nausea-inducing Patriot greeting, appreciated the tremendous source of free advertising that *Foreclosure Justice* had provided him and he was grateful as much as a man like Frimmer could express any gratitude. Left unsaid and unknown to Bravtart and the public was that Frimmer had just finished exacting revenge for Jason by quietly buying up shares of the Reality Now Network. He then had his newly installed CEO fire every executive and staff member involved with the canceling of *The Real Homeless of Malibu Beach*. Per his normal modus operandi, he sent out the word that the ingrates were to be blackballed. Just to make the point, Frimmer had his public relations bureaus leak rumors to RAP-friendly rumor bloggers on his payroll that two of the executives were being investigated by local militias for politically contributing to un-Real American, liberal candidates. Their careers in Hollywood were finished and within a few weeks, it was common but whispered knowledge that "Big Stake" had struck again, even though there no fingerprints to be found.

"It was courageous to show the poor as cockroaches infecting everything. When you are ready to do something big, let's talk," Frimmer blurted out before hanging up. Jason handed the phone back to the odd little man who then disappeared into the crowd.

Jason had been encouraged that night by Frimmer's backing, but as the idea drought continued, Jason was losing confidence and feared that history was racing by and leaving him behind. He was afraid that Frimmer might forget who he was and not return his calls or e-messages. He need not have worried. Jason would learn that Frimmer never forgot, never lost track of sources or talent he could exploit.

Jason's outlook was fully transformed a few weeks later on June 15, 2017 when he awoke promptly at 3:47 a.m. and had the first feeling of true revelation. As the day progressed and he started to mentally envision what became the Execution Channel, he told Sandy "it fell so easily into place that I was overcome with joy and a surging adrenaline of genius." He worked obsessively for 52 hours straight, fueled by gallons of black market superboost energy drinks from Instajolt, which had been one of the first advertisers to back *Foreclosure Justice*. When Jason finished the initial outline and exploitation fundamentals for the Execution Channel, he was overwhelmed by spiritual gravity. He walked briskly to the foyer of his mansion and kneeled before a 7-foot statue of Ayn Rand that Sandy had bought him as an anniversary present. He began to pray to the goddess of Real American liberty.

He began to sob in appreciation and remembered reading *Atlas Shrugged* for the first time as a 15-year-old prep school student in New England. He devoured the book in what he later said was a fever state and for days and days he experienced powerful dreams of destruction and creation and overwhelming surges of untamed narcissism. He had found a meaning to life, a new way of thinking about everything, a compass that now pointed True Jason. When he completed *Atlas Shrugged*, he felt totally liberated and transformed, cleansed of all existential doubt about his place in the universe. He also was sexually aroused to the point of ecstatic masturbation and then he dedicated his life to one unshakable truth – "Every day I shall build a monument to my genius."

Oh my Rand, he said to himself as the genius of the Execution Channel became clear to him, this is the same rush of pure self-interest and genius he felt then as a teenager. He imagined he felt what Dagny Taggart felt when she crash landed in Colorado and awoke in Galt's Gulch. He saw himself as a new hero of the ages, a creator of something transformative such as Rearden metal or Galt's magic motor.

Jason knew he was on the right track and nothing could stop him if strong men and women of like minds would back his idea. "So this is what it feels like to change the course of history," Jason said. Maybe it was time, he also thought, to give Penelope the benefit of the doubt.

CHAPTER THREE

PRAISE THE WAR ON THE POOR

"If people don't die from lack of health care and children don't starve, we can't create inspiring tales of innovation and economic development that leads to prosperity for all. It's time for the poor to stop taking, to stop whining about their plight and to stop expecting taxpayer-financed gifts. They need to make more sacrifices to boost morale for our Guardians of Galt."

– Gov. Lawrence C. Bowie, Real American Republic of Texas

B owie wasted no time in testing out his new powers. His first step was an easy and popular one when he rebranded the state name to the Real American Republic of Texas. He then ordered the capital moved from the "traitorous liberal viper's nest" of Austin to the Dallas suburb of Irving. When he made a bundle in real estate and construction kickbacks from the relocation, RAP business analysts hailed his entrepreneurial vision and said that Texans should applaud his leadership in showing how the Galtian Imperatives work best.

Bowie's greatest accomplishment during those first 90 days in office was, of course, his War on the Poor program of tax reforms. To pay for his bold measure of eliminating all business taxes and property taxes for people earning over 195,000 RAC a year, he pushed the RAP-dominated legislature in early 2017 to pass the War on the Poor package of tax initiatives. He was called a genius by RAP national policy leaders because his proposals were considered refreshingly simple – Bowie taxed the poor at a 90 percent rate for the first 10,000 RAC earned, 80 percent for the next 10,000 RAC earned, 70 percent for the next 10,000 RAC and so on. He had sales taxes increased by 10 percent for those earning less than 50,000 RAC. Bowie's plan exempted jets, yachts, armored vehicles, and homes costing over one million RAC "to spur economic growth and reward money-making geniuses for their obvious genius." Before Bowie had a law passed to eliminate unemployment payments, he had them reduced to 75 RAC a week and contingent on signing a RAP loyalty oath.

"Patriots, this War on the Poor initiative is necessary to correct decades of taxpayer waste and the coddling of moochers and takers. We know that being poor is not a handicap but rather a motivational asset, a state of mind and nothing else. Our tax system has been skewed far too long against the job creators, innovators and Guardians of Galt. The only gifts we should give out must be to those who abide by the Galtian Imperatives. It is time we help the unemployed and the so-called poor not with handouts like unemployment, which leads to moocherism, but by making sure they pay their fair share and have skin in the game. The poor need to be incentivized to realize their potential and embrace their role of creating prosperity for all. They themselves will likely not be touched by the prosperity but with this innovative, highly regressive plan, we give them the proper incentives to work and earn more. And to those who dare criticize this approach, I say the math is very simple – the more money you earn, the less in taxes you will pay. If we truly value our Guardians of Galt, their tax burden must be eliminated because they have earned and deserve an uneven playing field," Bowie said in a widely praised speech to the Dallas chapter of the Real American Chamber of Commerce.

When Bowie launched his War on the Poor campaign, he said it was inspired by "a glorious God who protects my riches and yours." Yet, even he was surprised about how active a role God was taking on his behalf. Within months, 10 RAP-led states enacted War on the Poor laws and variations. Bowie was credited with creating the Real American Citizen Tax template that drew praise and fierce protest across the increasingly divided country. And it didn't matter that the tax system ended up driving more states deeper into debt and a few into bankruptcy. What mattered is that political leaders and all Real Americans felt great doing it the right way by paying homage to the Galtian Imperatives.

Bowie was vilified by the usual moocher suspects for his far-reaching War on the Poor vision. "This is class warfare at its most naked and shows that Gov. Bowie has no grasp of math or morality. Does this man have no decency, no compassion?" said the Rev. Bob Washington, who led a coaltion of groups in RART to protest Bowie's "outrageous policies designed to punish the poor and vulnerable while benefiting his filthy rich friends." Bowie called out the recently-formed RART militia to forcefully break up the protests of community action organizations and former labor unions who had taken to the streets.

"Of course this is class warfare and you can bet that Real Americans want to be on the right side of that struggle instead of this pampered collection of parasites unfamiliar with the correct path of the Galtian Imperatives," Bowie said in response to Rev. Washington's accusations. "The good reverend should stick to tending his flock and leave the real work to us who strive each day to save our good republic from the contaminating ideas of his ilk."

He barely paused and doubled down on his War on the Poor campaign. In 2017, after the Liberty Court (formerly the U. S. Supreme Court) reversed itself and declared the national health-care reforms passed in 2010 unconstitutional. In its decision, The Liberty Court set precedence by mentioning the Galtian Imperatives and rejected the health care law passed by President Burt Octavian as "a liberty-denying affront to the vitality of the Galtian imperatives." Bowie led the charge in nullifying more federal laws by first making Medicaid requirements so stringent that no human being could qualify. Then he eliminated health care and food stamps for the poor altogether, calling it "a gift to the undeserving." Bowie then wisely redirected Medicaid and food stamps funding from the federal government to balance the state budget.

"These programs that give away health care and food to the so-called poor have created an evil sense of entitlement that has sucked away at the moral and economic core of our great land," Bowie said on The Austerity Factor, the popular RAP Network political talk show. "If people don't die from lack of health care and children don't starve, we can't create inspiring tales of innovation and economic development that leads to prosperity for all. It's time for the poor to stop taking, to stop whining about their plight and expecting taxpayer-financed gifts. They need to make more sacrifices to boost morale for our Guardians of Galt."

Bowie also set trends in selling off state government, piece by piece. State libraries and museums were given away to campaign contributors who began charging admission or selling off the collections. "Taxpayers expect us to be wise. Books are dead materials and unworthy of taxpayer subsidy. Taxpayers must not support paintings and other examples of decadent art that do nothing but hang on a wall or sit there," he said in a press statement.

Get your corporate sponsor

In another revenue-raising innovation, Bowie sold the Real American Republic of Texas university system to Chinese and Russian investors. This in turn became an innovative investment scheme bubble to sell off individual schools, academic departments and even tenured faculty members who were amazed to find out that an emergency decree had made them "assets to be sold, traded or fired with no notice." Only the University of Texas football program was spared as Bowie deemed it "an irreplaceable state asset on par with the Alamo."

Bowie's state government restructuring showed the benefit of putting everything up for sale. After an emergency redistricting decree eliminated three-quarters of the state assembly, he pushed through a law mandating that by 2019 the state's 9 senators and 29 assembly members had to find corporate sponsorships to cover their salaries, expenses, retirement plans, staff, health care lottery fees, and slush funds.

"We have already taken a decisive step to prove that in our new democracy, fewer voices in the legislature make for a more efficient, market-focused legislature. Now we take the next step to true accountability – we must sell or lease all our elective offices to the highest corporate bidder so the people of this great Republic will not have to pay one cent of salary for their elected leaders," said Bowie, who set a good example by signing a 10-year lease for the governor's office to Hudsucker Oil for 100.6 million RAC. "This is the wave of the future. We know the legislature has been bought and sold on a regular basis but it's time to make it official and transparent. If a politician can't find sufficient corporate support, then they have been vetted just right and they have no business representing the crucial interests of our exalted Guardians of Galt. And if those politicians don't live up to the contract demands with their corporate sponsor, they can be fired and replaced at will. This is far more efficient than the time and cost of actual voting."

Bowie said his annual multi-million RAC salary was earned because of his talents as a shrewd negotiator and visionary who had cut the size of the RART government by more than half. By emergency executive order he fired more than 126,320 teachers, government workers, secretaries, public defenders, police officers, fire department personnel, judges, court clerks, prosecutors, meat and environmental inspectors and financial accountants.

"Only the moochers will panic and cower in fear. Fiscal responsibility and enforcing austerity are our top priorities. Everything else can be handled better and efficiently by having faith in our Randian free market system," Bowie said during an RAP prayer service announcing the mass layoffs. By emergency executive order, he also cut by 33 percent the salaries of 622 government workers who didn't have business subsidy deals. Bowie did hire and give raises to the 172 state-paid workers who were labeled "essential workers," tasked with the marketing, public relations and sales functions necessary to dismantle the RART government.

Not everything went smoothly. Shoot-outs at motor vehicle registration licensing departments became regular events as private vendors charged more than 200 RAC just to see a worker, another 150 RAC to pay a quality processing fee for quick service and then 400 RAC to get the right documents. Altogether, prices went up 1,020 percent and Bowie hailed the change as "necessary and welcome to real free-market loving people." Even the brand name and staff of the Texas Rangers, the most valued and vaunted of Texas lawmen institutions, was sold to a Russian consortium, which Bowie defended as "regrettable but necessary to balance our budget and give welcome tax rebates to our Guardians of Galt."

When smog alerts in RART became a daily occurrence due to the elimination of all clean air regulations, a Bowie spokesperson said the alerts were based on faulty science and that a 122-car, 35-death freeway pile up outside of Dallas that many blamed on heavy smog was little more "than an unfortunate incident that had nothing to do with dirty air."

When a group of Texas mayors complained about the elimination of revenue sharing from state government, Bowie at first ignored them. When the mayors warned the public about rising crime rates because police departments had been virtually eliminated and force-depleted fire departments had to let too many houses and commercial buildings burn to the ground, Bowie gave them a lesson in tough love. "These whiner mayors are stuck in defunct ways of thinking. When their cities decay enough, Galtian solutions will emerge to fit the market need," Bowie said. "Real Americans need to take security into their hands and practice self-reliance. They can shoot looters in their homes or on the streets and put out their own fires instead of depending on wasteful and inefficient publicly created entities to save the day."

With the RAP wave reaching a crest of popularity and widespread austerity being embraced throughout Real America, many believed that Bowie was now on a fast track to the presidency in 2020, if not of a fractured United States than of the 15-member New Southern Alliance, which had emerged as a popular governing alternative for RAP-dominated states.

It was said in many political circles that Bowie, like Lincoln in 1860, was the only candidate who could unite and save the country by eventually eliminating government altogether. But Bowie had to prove his strength and win re-election as RART governor in 2018 to prove his long-term mettle. And that re-election was anything but assured because he was running against Col. Rufus T. Fairbush, the most powerful militia leader in Real America. It promised to be a primary fight for the ages because Fairbush was determined to take Bowie down by the ballot or the bullet.

CHAPTER FOUR

THE BIRTH OF THE EXECUTION CHANNEL

"We are meeting two vital objectives: viable and sustaining economic development and a public reckoning to right the wrongs of Real American history through a fair and balanced execution process in which guilt and innocence are less important than maximum profit capabilities."

– JASON BRAVTART

In 2018 after The Execution Channel was successfully launched, Jason was debriefed about the genesis of his idea by investigators he thought were from the RAP Bureau of Real American Investigation. He was told the interviews would be part of the official record to chronicle this greatest of economic achievements in Real America.

Jason was happy to oblige and told all. He called the breakthrough a bolt of Galtian genius. "I wanted to restart the motors of the world," he said. As he looked back on the fateful day in June 2017, he remembered clearly the sun struggling to break through the morning haze of air pollution as he finished his morning run. He said he awoke highly energized that morning at 3:47 and during his run he felt something was about to break.

"Praise to Galt," Sandra said as she kissed him goodbye before leaving for work as chief marketing officer for the 1st John Galt SoCal Militia. "Keep the faith and you will break through as Penelope prophesized. Today might be the day."

Most of all he remembered a towel over his legs after his run was cut short to due to a heavy smog morning and sporadic sniper fire. He could still see the three seemingly unrelated stories that were on the front page of the Real American Webwire. "At the bottom of the screen, I saw the headline that Texas had executed three criminals in two days. At the top of the screen, the headline said the Liberty Court had abolished the death penalty appeal process. I thought 'well, that's going to lead to a lot more executions.' And then just below it, I read a column about how 44 states were struggling to balance their budgets because the poor weren't paying their fair share of taxes," Jason said. "The idea then hit me like a thunderbolt."

Jason didn't believe in coincidence. Every second of every day built a person's ladder of destiny, he believed. Just as John Galt had persevered through trial and tribulation and government torture designed to crush him and eliminate his spirit, Jason felt his exile had served a purpose and prepared him to seize his destiny at just the right time. "Really, I didn't consciously connect the stories at first. They connected to me," he told investigators. As a propaganda producer, Jason said it was a quick leap to imagine the power, majesty and immense profitability of live executions on the televinet.

"I had an incredible, overflowing surge of adrenaline all the way down to my toes. I knew immediately this was big, this would change the course of Real American history and make a lot of money," Jason told his interrogators Rick and Charlie (no second names were given and none were asked for). It had potential, Jason continued, to be a massive windfall for investors, the states, and any network brave enough to embrace the concept. Jason was certain the show, which he tentatively titled *Final Justice Live*, would be the biggest reality televinet show of them all, maybe even the most popular show of all time.

Jason figured there would be no problem with the supply of condemned prisoners because cooperating states would have a financial incentive for more executions to meet public demand. There could be publicly financed execution sites, larger televinet contracts and greater marketing opportunities to possibly unite the country for a common good as foretold by the Galtian Imperatives. If everything worked out, public skepticism about public executions would give way to increased acceptance and demand for a greater number of public executions and more states would use this as an incentive to restore and expand capital punishment laws.

"It combines death with financial opportunity," Jason said at the first advertising presentation for The Execution Channel. He also talked in admiration about the genius of the Romans who gave their citizens bread, circuses, and gladiator bouts to the death, crucifixions and lions devouring Christians. Participating states that showed innovation and enthusiasm would share in greater glory and profits. The early adapter states would be rewarded with set fees and a larger cut of profits. He suspected that some advertisers might be skittish at first but then would quickly jump on board. Jason knew he would have no problem whipping up the publicity machine. He imagined Execution Days with scores of executions nationally to make it into a country-wide experience.

"Don't you feel the societal need, a hunger for revenge and justice that needs to be satisfied?" Jason later said in a speech before an appreciative audience of the Real American Republic of Texas Chamber of Commerce after the official franchise launch of The Execution Channel in the spring of 2018. "For decades our country was subverted by liberal heretics and saboteurs. We are meeting two vital objectives: viable and sustaining economic development and a public reckoning to right the wrongs of Real American history. We will have a fair and balanced execution process in which guilt and innocence are less important than maximum profit capabilities."

Going bold

Jason needed to move quickly because, like any inventor, he figured an idea this obvious couldn't remain secret for long. It took an agonizing two days for Jason to finally connect with James "Big Stake" Frimmer but he told the interrogators that he used the time well to formulate a winning presentation. Rather than create a digital presentation, piece by piece he put together a hand-written chart that he put on the wall of his home office. He wanted this to be tangible, to be felt and seen and he later commissioned an artist to paint a portrait of the history-altering wall display.

Final Justice Live was the working title for the show but Jason told his interrogators that he moved beyond the original outline to something much grander, the history-changing Execution Channel that would eventually captivate the world. He would dispense with finding the right network and simply create his own. "I felt like John Galt when he realized that his genius could not be confined by convention," Jason wrote in his digital diary, an entry that the agents later put in their report.

It didn't take long for Jason to determine that the key to success was to get one state in as an early, enthusiastic and experimental adapter. Jason immediately thought of the Real American Republic of Texas and he was a huge fan of Gov. Lawrence T. "Demon Seed" Bowie whose legendary incoherence had vaulted him into national prominence. Jason remembered Bowie was the cover boy of a mainstream national newsmagazine a year earlier that proclaimed him a 21st century Huey Long and the "RAP savior who gives Galtian corporate populism a strident voice."

"I had been impressed by Gov. Bowie's leadership and vision and liked how he handled the situation in Houston," Jason said about what many believed was a defining moment for Bowie. When 78 men, women, and children died over a three-day period from a water contamination outbreak in Houston after the explosion of a chemical plant, Bowie didn't issue a statement through a spokesman – he stood up at a press conference of carefully vetted repbloggers and took credit for a job well done. Bowie declared "double martial law" to keep order in Houston and showed his pride in a state that was leading the way in environmentally related deaths.

be the mysterious will of God that explains why the environment continues to act funny but that should not stop us from maximum exploitation of natural resources," Bowie had said. "Come on folks, let's stop being chicken little types and whining pussies around here. People die all the time but we can't forget there's money to be made and opportunities gained by showing good horse sense in not worrying about what we can't control. We shouldn't coddle future generation from the consequences of our excesses because full-scale environmental degradation is a wonderful economic development platform. We have made progress in removing all barriers to prosperity by ridding ourselves of hateful regulations that defy common sense and wreck countless good money-making schemes."

Bowie was hailed throughout Real America for the searing honesty of what came next. "These deaths in Houston were sacrifices made in the cause of prosperity for all. We can't blame shrewd industrialists if small mishaps like this lead to collateral damage and untimely deaths of people who, let us be frank about this, should live in better neighborhoods." In an appearance a few days later on Counterstrike, the Galt News Channel's top-rated political talk show, Bowie said he was taking proactive action on environmental issues by ordering the last remaining environmental agency employee to stop issuing smog and toxic spill alerts.

A week later, Bowie fired the employee for telling a foreign reporter from the anti-Galtian political zone of Vermont that the number of dead in Houston had grown to 5,186 and was rising daily. Entire neighborhoods had been wiped out by a toxic cloud and private, untrained militia forces had been unable to cope with the aftermath and became casualties themselves. "Telling the truth is no defense. This employee has been terminated and arrested for conduct detrimental to Real American values," Bowie said.

Jason and Sandy Bravtart had seen the report on Bowie's brave stand in Houston on the Real American Network Evening News and they were moved by his example. "He's just the right man to make the Execution Channel a reality," Jason said to Sandy. "He proves the truth of the Galtian Imperatives and what glory there is in putting them to work for prosperity for all," Sandy added.

"I hadn't had the pleasure of meeting Gov. Bowie but I knew we shared a Galtian vision of prosperity, progress and money-making zeal," Jason said at the debriefing. He suspected Frimmer could make the introduction but Jason also knew he had to be ready to hit the ground running from day one. "Mr. Frimmer wasn't going to waste time on a half-baked plan. He could make things happen fast if he wanted," he said.

Jason told his interrogators the plan from grew from a pay-per-view model to a full-fledged network and brand name. He started to envision what became the Execution Night in America standard of time blocks not unlike the same successful formula developed by professional football savants to grab and maintain audience share. Jason imagined a nightly menu of options for viewers: pre- and post-execution analysis programs; medical experts to describe the physiological details of death by execution; psychologists to offer scientific evidence that public executions were valuable in enhancing society's well-being; political commentary; documentaries to provide historical re-enactments of popular and innovative execution methods throughout the centuries; audience interviews and special RAP SocMedia platforms to tap; and crews to capture the moment-by-moment reactions of the families of victims and even, perhaps, the families of the ExSub, the executed subject.

Jason said he couldn't stop his genius from flowing and the rush of solid gold ideas kept coming. He imagined a daily news program, Execution Central, to preview coming attractions and keep up with legal developments and to show the running tally about how government coffers and private sector Guardians of Galt were being enhanced by the Execution Channel.

Overcoming a fatal flaw

But as the Execution Channel concept continued to evolve, Jason said he knew there was a flaw, perhaps a fatal flaw, which could undermine the entire enterprise – the severe visual limitations to the current execution methods in place. "The cramped death chamber environment found in every prison was mostly dark and unhelpful for full exploitative purposes. And the lethal injection method preferred by most states was visually boring and offered little excitement to viewers. After all, who wanted to watch a condemned prisoner, a murderer or rapist or serial killer or anti-RAP traitor, feel a twinge of pain, sigh and go to sleep?" Jason said. "It was Sandy who figured out what to do."

Sandra had been blown away by Jason's genius in the past and it was the same, if not more so with his idea for the Execution Channel. The first time he outlined the genius of the Execution Channel, she was overcome with excitement and insisted on an "all-out, makes my ears pop fuck" in their outdoor Jacuzzi. When Jason told her of the flaw that could undermine the potential glory of the Execution Channel, she cut through the doubt with and quickly saw what he needed. "Sandy came to my rescue," he said.

"I'm sure you would have gotten there on your own but really all you need to do is think outdoor stadiums and outdoor executions. What could be more natural or profitable than public death?" said. "It also wouldn't hurt to have some blood and gore or at least an outc tric chair and hanging or firing squads," she said as freckles brightened. "Once Sandy got going, you couldn't stop her." Jason remembered.

"You could make executions fun and family-friendly, an educational experience and part of our Real American civic duty like visiting the RealAmerica Land theme park. You could have video highlights of arrests and confessions and interrogations put on the big screens in the stadium," Sandy had said. "Remember I told you a while ago about how we started to put edited interrogations of anti-Galt subversives on our paid subscription web site? We called it our Trial by Ordeal option and well, it took a while to get going because it was the first of its kind. But just in the past few weeks, it has exploded in popularity because people can't seem to get enough of the water dunking and electric shock-induced confessions. We even include a 24/7 camera at one of our reeducation camps so patriots can keep track of their favorite subversive. We are also planning to include online-feedback for suggestions on what kind of interrogation excesses they would like tried on their favorite subversive. The public is ready, far more ready than I thought, for a greater range of alternative entertainment choices. Honey, you have seen this future and its money-making capability. It's sheer genius."

Jason said he became overcome with joy. "This was the final missing piece: a wide variety of executions in public financed stadiums for private sector gain," he explained. "Sandy was so right. This concept born of genius and opportunity deserved the largest stage possible."

Sandy got very excited as she estimated that their personal cash flow concerns would be solved for good. "This wasn't just about money it was also about power," Jason said to his interrogators. "She also dreamed of creating and leading her own militia brigade and figured the lawless southwest sector was a good place to start. Sandy had vision and wanted to buy a town in western New Mexico that had declared bankruptcy and was looking for a buyer. We had dreamed of buying a large piece of land, a city or county or maybe even an off-shore island, to build the perfect Galtian enclave, one that would inspire the world and change history."

Jason had one more thing to add to the record. Their brainstorming had aroused Sandy. She needed relief and told her genius husband, "Let's fuck again until my ears pop."

CHAPTER FIVE
THE FAIRBUSH DILEMMA

"We want not only to eliminate government.
We want to eliminate the idea of government once and for all."

– COL. RUFUS T. FAIRBUSH,
CHAIRMAN OF THE MILITIA COMMITTEE OF REAL AMERICAN PATRIOTS,
GREATER TEXAS CHAPTER

acronyms are funny

We began this tale with reference to Gov. Bowie's political fix. Actually, there were two major roadblocks threatening his political destiny by the middle of 2017. First, Bowie was in a financial quagmire of his own making because the actual returns of the War on the Poor scheme didn't match his faith-based expectations. He fired his first budget alchemist when he was told that revenues were 80 percent below projections. He fired the next budget alchemist when that man's projections showed it to be even worse than 80 percent.

"The math has to work. What do you mean the poor don't make enough to pay their fair share?" he yelled at the next budget alchemist who was ordered to make the numbers work. Bowie needed the poor share revenue because he had promised his business sponsors a piece of the action from the 14.75 billion RAC Real American Texas Free Market Enterprise Slush Fund. Bowie controlled RATFMESF disbursements and gave out grants and zero-interest loans with few questions asked to large businesses that pledged fidelity to the Galtian Imperatives and promised to create "prosperity for all" while they gave a 15 percent kickback fee to Bowie.

RATFMESR ran on an honor system that required no oversight verification or accountability, and Bowie trumpeted this innovation to eliminate bureaucratic red tape as a "Galtian virtue that will go far in calming business anxiety." It was believed by business analysts that if Bowie's business benefactors in the oil, banking, gun running, black-market

pharmaceutical, pornography, prostitution, slave labor, body a...
personal finance exploitation industries lost confidence in his abil.
properly finance RATFMESF, they could find someone else who could.

His second concern was more daunting and life-threatening. Bowie was being pushed by radicalized Real American Party cadres who wanted more action and in Col. Rufus T. Fairbush, he had a real opponent with the muscle and desire to take him out. Fairbush, the Real American Militia commander in the San Antonio district and chairman of the influential Militia Committee of Real American Patriots of Greater Texas, had declared his candidacy to run against Bowie in the Real American Party gubernatorial primary in 2018. Fairbush announced his intention one hour after Bowie was sworn in as governor. Fairbush hated Bowie and wanted the governor out of the picture. "I want to primary his ass out of existence because he lacks purity of vision," Fairbush said at a meeting of advisors. "Bowie doesn't have the stomach to tame the moocher underclass once and for all. That's the same as being a traitor to the cause."

Fairbush was not a man to be trifled with and had a reputation as a ruthless political player. Fairbush had appointed himself a militia colonel but the record showed he had been dishonorably discharged as a clerk-typist private from the U. S. Army decades earlier for his pro-militia advocacy and his call to kill liberals, IRS agents, officials from the United Nations, ATF agents, and any military officers who didn't agree with his "liberty" agenda. He was elected county sheriff five times on the successful, single-minded platform of "I will shoot down government tyranny."

Fairbush made good on his campaign promise when he garnered national attention in 2014 by killing two FBI agents on his property. The agents had come to investigate allegations of gun running, racketeering, providing lethal explosive materials and training for abortion clinic bombers, leading a special militia to carry out terrorist attacks against the United States and using his sheriff's office to run a protection racket in his county. Fairbush claimed self-defense "against government tyranny and trespassing" for shooting the agents in the back and was acquitted by a jury of his peers. His myth as a second-to-none patriot leader only grew and Fairbush had his sights set on taking out Bowie.

"Bowie has too much of a collectivist taint for our liking. He refuses to enforce the anti-moocher sanctions our forefathers fought and died for. He just doesn't get it. We want not only to eliminate government, we want to eliminate the idea of government once and for all," Fairbush proclaimed in a nationally televised speech before a meeting of New Southern Alliance religious leaders in September 2017 as the Execution Channel was in the planning stages. "We shouldn't have to remind Gov. Bowie of this uncompromising truth very often and no so-called public execution scheme can change the unalterable facts of this election."

Bowie had no problem translating Fairbush's shot across his bow. If Bowie didn't or couldn't finish the job of eliminating the idea of government and putting more liberals, moochers and takers in prison, Fairbush was saying that he would.

Fairbush was building on political momentum from his decision in late 2016 to send his militia forces to southern and southwest Texas to take on the cabal of Russian and Mexican drug armies who had made territorial grabs in those regions. The famous Battle of Van Horn became part of Fairbushian lore and Fairbush declared victory after two days of battle. Like Bowie, Fairbush had a tentative grasp on the truth and intrepid investigators later determined that it was in actuality a truce as both sides agreed that any more bloodshed was bad for business. Investigating agents later learned that Fairbush was rewarded with hefty financial payouts from the drug czars for drugs to be transported through his spheres of influence.

Fairbush also became a favorite of samestream media pundits who admired him for his bold and uncompromising policy stands. He said slavery should be revived to help job creators maximize prosperity and he demanded reparations with interest from the federal government to the families of American slave holders whose slaves were freed at the end of the Civil War. "We hear too much about reparations for the descendants of so-called slaves. What about that lost by the owners? Where was the respect for private property? Property is property no matter how you slice it and this property was seized by a cowardly and murderous Yankee government that offered no compensation," Fairbush said at a public rally of the recently formed Confederacy Revival League in early 2017.

Fairbush considered democracy a cancer because it offered bad lessons about equal opportunity and equal access and this led to some creative maneuvers by some Fairbush followers. Bowie's security forces foiled three assassination attempts, including one close call when Bowie's bodyguards shot and blew up a Fairbush soldier wearing a suicide bomb vest after he breached the security at the Bowie Ranch outside of Dallas. Bowie had publicly dismissed the incidents as the acts of a "few deranged citizens" but privately he was concerned. He took to wearing a holstered pair of submachine guns at all times under his suit jacket and did not make his schedule public out of concerns that he could find himself caught in an ambush or tracked down by Fairbush's surveillance drones.

Bowie watched with apprehension as Fairbush's "Alamo" militia division became the largest in RART. According to blog-net reports, this militia group was responsible for killing more than 1,300 illegal liberals and immigrants who tried flee from Texas before paying the RART passport exit fee. Fairbush's militia was also the best-equipped such unit in Real America, courtesy of a peaceful seizure of a federal army post and confiscation of its supplies in December 2016 after the RAP took control nationally. The seizure came about after months of negotiations between renegade Army officers and Fairbush and it led to similar seizures of U. S. military installations across Real American Party-dominated states in 2017.

Fairbush promised never to take the rank of general because he believed only God almighty deserved that rank. He commanded a tank brigade, a helicopter squadron, artillery, missiles, two infantry battalions, 35 drone aircraft (including 12 with missile firing capacity) and a black operations unit that set up operations near the state capital and had Bowie under constant surveillance. It was common knowledge that Fairbush's Alamo Liberty Foundation had imposed a creative protection racket in southwest Texas under the guise of "common defense" fees. Bowie was concerned that the Alamo Liberty Foundation was being funded by some of Bowie's closest business benefactors. Bowie knew they were being smart and were hedging their bets.

"If we don't watch out, Fairbush will have me out-moneyed, out-manned and out-gunned and damn well out-surrounded," Bowie told his military advisors after Fairbush announced an alliance with militia groups in the border states of Oklahoma, New Mexico, Louisiana and Arkansas.

Frimmer to the rescue

When it came to dealing with Fairbush, Bowie initiated some undercover operations in 2017 but he was unsure when or even if these infiltration efforts would work. Socblog mercenary teams for both camps flooded the televinet with escalating attacks of rumors and character assassination accusations. Bowie's manhood and honor were challenged daily (he was accused of having deep, latent homosodomonic desires and wealth redistribution fantasies) and Fairbush was accused of consulting directly with space aliens and dead 19th-century gunfighters for guidance. Spokesmen for both Bowie and Fairbush promised to exact justice and vengeance from the socblog perpetrators for their insults. There were rumors of a massacre of a Bowie-financed blogging platoon by Fairbush's agents which Bowie denied.

Bowie knew a stalemate situation would favor Fairbush and that was unsettling. As the pace of killings and televinet warfare attacks increased, Bowie told an aide "I hear said that in the long run, everyone dies. I know Fairbush wants to shorten my long run by a whole lot."

As with Jason Bravtart, the tides of fate started to shift in Bowie's favor. Bowie was pondering his political fate when the RAP-led Liberty Court offered him an opportunity to change the dynamic. For years, Texas and other states that were now in the New Southern Alliance had called for eliminating all automatic death penalty appeals and the Liberty Court settled the matter once and for all. After the RAP congressional coup of 2017 led to the rapid impeachment of three liberal, "anti-Real American" justices, the Liberty Court moved fast to ratify the RAP agenda. By an 8-1 vote, the Liberty Court agreed with Texas and seven other RAP states saying "there is nothing cruel and unusual about letting states determine their own appeal methodology. Justice delayed is justice denied is a state's rights issue that demands precedence despite quaint notions about due process." The court also ruled that appeal delays were "economically inefficient and contrary to the Galtian Imperatives." (RAP leaders in the House immediately launched impeachment proceedings against the token Liberty Court liberal who had dissented from the ruling and called it "a barbaric perversion.")

When the Liberty Court made its decision on capital punishment, the Real American Republic of Texas was already executing on average three criminals a week, but Bowie was glad he could pick up the pace. It could be a timely public distraction and might even keep Fairbush in his place for a while until other plans could be put in place.

Bowie felt a whole lot better a few weeks later when he got a late-night phone call from James "Big Stake" Frimmer, the most feared and reclusive billionaire in Real America. Frimmer, the CEO and chairman of Frimmer Empire Enterprises, hadn't been seen in public since 1982 and there were rumors aplenty that Frimmer had actually been dead for years and replaced by a group of private equity speculators who spoke in his name. Frimmer did exist and enjoyed using his vast public relations machine to spread rumors highlighting his existence or nonexistence to an endless supply of gullible reporters, bloggers and commentators.

Bowie didn't know how Frimmer discovered the number of a special phone he reserved only for his mistresses but Bowie didn't ask questions. Frimmer, Bowie thought, was like a real life Wizard of Oz, the corporate icon of icons, one who did happen to know and could see all. As usual when speaking to subordinates, Frimmer didn't waste many words as he told Bowie about a surefire-winning business opportunity called the Execution Channel. Frimmer said it was the brainchild of the renowned political reality televinet producer Jason Bravtart. Bowie knew Bravtart was a true Real American innovator in the arts of propaganda and political assassination and Bowie had been a devoted fan of his award-winning hit show *Foreclosure Justice.*

"Bravtart says this will change the course of Real American history as we know it. I think the kid is exaggerating but we need a state to take a leading role and you would be a damn fool not to jump on board. There's significant RAC to be made," said Frimmer, a financial speculator who was rumored to have driven a "big stake," sometimes liter-

ally and sometimes metaphorically, through the hearts of com
people who displeased him for any number of reasons.

Though they had never met in person, Frimmer had been the top financial backer in Bowie's rise to the top and Bowie didn't know exactly
how much he was in Frimmer's debt. Through various not-for-profit
organizations and political reaction committees, Frimmer was able to
launder money and channel campaign funds to candidates without leaving any fingerprints. Bowie had done a lot to advance Frimmer's agenda
and he felt honored that he was in Frimmer's pocket, that he was one of
the few political leaders around whom Frimmer talked to directly, that
he was a commodity being held in reserve for maximum exploitation.

It was all too good to be true and Bowie resisted the urge to act like
an overexcited puppy dog because Bowie believed, not without reason,
that Frimmer was a man of real power, a life-and-death decision maker who dealt out consequences and moved markets before his first cup
of morning coffee. Despite unlimited reserves of self-delusion, Bowie
knew his political power, like his physical being, was merely transitory
when compared to the immense, God-like power exerted by Frimmer.

Bowie hyperventilated when he imagined himself a real business ac-
complice with Frimmer. Among many tales, it was common but un-
proven knowledge that Frimmer had quietly engineered the change to
Real American Currency and enhanced his legend when it was rumored
he made tens of billions RAC in a few days by ruthlessly manipulating RAC value. For its shadowy efforts, FEE had been hailed by many
commentators in the RAP media complex as a "true Guardian of Galt"
corporation that validated the Galtian Imperatives of maximum exploitation of public good and fidelity to nothing but one's genius.

Bowie listened closely. He wasn't trusted enough yet to hear all the details but he was smart enough to realize the reality televinet concept of the Execution Channel was a winning idea whose time had come. Moreover, Bowie knew immediately that public executions for fun, private profit and public entertainment value could solve many of his political and financial problems at once. Bowie's head spun at the amount of honest kickbacks he could grab while balancing the RART budget at the same time. There would be more than enough to support a major increase in his own militia – it would be nice to have his own squadron of missile-firing drones, he thought – and counter Fairbush's rise while helping Bowie finance the lifestyles of two ex-wives, one current wife, six children, and two mistresses.

"I'm ready. What do you need?" Bowie enthusiastically asked.

"We are still in the planning stage but first, grab some land around the capital region and cook up state financing for a public execution stadium. Call it an economic development grant or whatever you want. The stadium should seat 60,000, maybe as much as 80,000 fans. Make it a dome so we can close the roof on bad air days and open up when the toxic clouds disperse."

"I'll get right on it," Bowie said.

"Second," Frimmer continued, "We are planning for many types of executions the public will demand and my people have already set up focus groups. The preliminary list says hangings, electrocutions, firing squads, gas chambers, beheadings, human-devouring lions, burning at the stake, or being torn apart by a specialty breed of man-, woman- and child-killing Rottweilwolfs."

Bowie was impressed by the quantity and quality of execution choices.

"Third, I need you to keep your damn fool mouth shut and don't tell anyone what the land and stadium are for. Just do it and wait for further instructions."

"Can do," Bowie said.

"You had better 'can do' Bowie. We need to move fast because this idea is so obvious I'm surprised it hasn't been done. And immediately halt this mistress dilly-dallying nonsense. We can't afford any sex scandals right now." Frimmer ended the call without saying goodbye.

As he took a deep breath after Frimmer hung up, Bowie felt energized. He didn't like the demand to dump his mistresses Maria and Brenda but it was necessary. His first thought was 'my legacy will be set' and he imagined the Execution Channel as his win-win track to a sizeable payday and a chance for historical greatness. He even felt confident that he could now confront Fairbush and win the primary war.

After the call with Bowie, Frimmer considered a different set of assumptions. Using an internal calculation only he understood, Frimmer decided that Bowie was near his peak maximum usefulness to him and it would only be a rapid descent into inefficient market mediocrity after that. When Frimmer mentioned this calculation to his top aide Roland Gunner, it was translated as Bowie would no longer be market efficient, he knew too many secrets and he would have to be resettled to Happy Meadows, a final resting ground for former Frimmer allies who had outlived their economic usefulness and enemies who had been up to no good. Frimmer decided to delay the details and timing of Gov. Bowie's departure until after the launch of the Execution Channel.

CHAPTER SIX

WHAT'S GOOD FOR FEE IS GOOD FOR REAL AMERICA

"It will be seen that they owed nothing to fortune but the opportunity which gave them matter to shape into what form they saw fit; and without that opportunity their powers would have been wasted, and without their powers the opportunity would have been in vain."

– MACHIAVELLI, THE PRINCE

J ames "Big Stake" Frimmer II was not a man to waste fortune or opportunity. He was the money man behind the Execution Channel and, according to initial press reports when rumors about the Execution Channel surfaced, the investment was an act of free market exploitation, a bid to corner a market that Frimmer himself was creating. When the Execution Channel was officially launched in the fall of 2017, a vice president for proactive public relations and manipulation at Frimmer Empire Enterprises was quoted as saying in a press release that Frimmer Empire Enterprises, or FEE, was making "a modest investment in the Execution Channel because of the good it will do for FEE. It's important to never forget that what's good for FEE is good for Real America."

FEE rarely issued press releases and in fact few Americans, Real or otherwise, knew or understood what FEE was and what it did. FEE had a fearsome reputation for making money and eliminating competitors. The amount of investment in the Execution Channel was left blank, as was the real reason Frimmer was involved but then Frimmer was good at keeping the world guessing. For decades, journalists and researchers and brave government regulators had attempted to figure out exactly what FEE was, the vastness of its influence, how it maintained its veneer of secrecy and whether Frimmer himself was alive.

While the world pondered the mystery of FEE, few disputed this fact – FEE backing meant that the Execution Channel was to be taken seriously. Frimmer also was doing what made him a successful speculator, ruthless financier and proud, unparalleled corruptor of public good. hedging his bets and keeping a tight rein on one of Execution Channel business partners, Gov. Bowie.

"Bowie is the most high profile moron and blowhard on my payroll, but he's more competent than not and happily does what he's been told," Frimmer told his Chief of Staff Roland Gunner. Bowie was known to deliver on demand. Frimmer made a no-risk financial killing when he used a Real American Republic of Texas treasury handout to subsidize the winning bid for the former federal interstate highway system in RAPT that Bowie had seized. Bowie rigged the bid for Frimmer, who made a 625 million RAC profit when he sold it to a consortium of Brazilian and South African investors within days without risking any of his own money.

Frimmer used that windfall to complete the purchase of three RAP-dominated state legislatures; six governors; 36 RAP members of Congress who promised to stop doing any work except to speak out loudly and frequently against anti-Galtian subversives; seven RAP U. S. senators who pledged to filibuster any law that interfered with Frimmer's business activities; and three federal cabinet chiefs – two were RAP members and the third was a part of the dying breed of conservative Republicans – who quietly erased any government reporting requirements for FEE on trivial matters such as money laundering, gun running, black market pharmaceutical sales, human trafficking, reporting human deaths, and wide scale water contamination from natural gas exploration on private and public lands.

And there was more, much more, to come. While Bowie and Bravtart both sought redemption and riches with the Execution Channel, Frimmer saw his cash investment of 1.45 billion RAC into the Execution Channel as a loss leader, a gateway into something much more significant – buying off the final pieces of the political puzzle from sea to shining sea. For decades he had invested hundreds of millions, first in dollars and then, even better in his mind, with worthless faith-based RAC, in buying off every politician he could and destroying those by every means possible who would not be bought or didn't remain bought after being bought.

Only Frimmer and a few of his closest advisors knew how well the plan was working. Those politicians on the payroll had passed amazingly effective bills to enact political loyalty and property/income level qualifications of voters in 19 states. Not surprisingly, each of those states with depleted voting pools elected politicians who wanted to join the right-thinking team of the Real American Party. Frimmer laughed when a growing chorus of business media pundits applauded the RAP for wanting to rig the electoral map and they didn't mention his name because they had no clue how big his influence was. "I don't want to rig anything. I want to own it," he told his numbers staff.

Frimmer seemed well on the way to owning it. Frimmer did not come up with the brilliant plans to change the Electoral College mathematics in 16 states – Octavian had carried 11 of those states in 2012 – that led to the Real American Party landslide in 2016. But he and a group of fellow billionaires funded the effort and Frimmer personally subsidized Bowie's traveling road show. Since he was doing little in Congress anyway, Bowie became the leader and enthusiastic evangelist of the effort in 2015 by Republican and Real American Party state legislatures to rig the elections and ensure permanent RAP dominance in the decades to come.

"We are proud to support the new mathematics. For our Real American vision to succeed, we must overcome the moocher majority through disenfranchising laws and creative gerrymandering. Our goal is to create moocher voting ghettos to let them have their vote and then to make sure those votes don't count for squadoosh," a mock said in testimony before a cheering Virginia state assembly committee. Altogether, Bowie traveled around the country and made more than $2 million in fees speaking in favor of "new mathematics we can understand and not one used by the liberal traitors to force their majority tyranny upon good, god-fearing Real Americans." Frimmer was proud of the "new mathematics" call to action, in part because it was he who had coined the phrase.

The various plans worked to perfection. In Texas, Bowie won by a 70 percent margin after the state employed 27 new voter suppression laws. On the national level, though the 2016 Democratic Party candidate Carrie Hilton won the popular vote by more than 8 million votes, the Republican Party candidate Anthony Ribinio won the Electoral College count by more than 120 votes. Hilton's supporters took to the streets and howled in protest, but the Galt Street Journal dismissed them "as losers and whiners who cannot accept the new mathematics of elections that were accomplished in a fair and balanced legal fashion. These states and the country as a whole have rejected the moocher and looter majority which threatened the Real American way of life."

Frimmer's Law of Business Expansion

In Frimmer's efficient way of doing business, once a subject was bought there was no getting out of being bought. It was a lifetime pledge that could even transcend death (Frimmer was implementing a new option to have the bought status transferred to either living family members or politicians who succeeded the departed). Even better, Frimmer had a statistical formula to determine a glorious end game – politicians addicted to Frimmer's money and ideological persuasion would eventually perform like trained circus animals and act without any financial inducements. Frimmer planned to slowly withdraw the bribery fixes as politicians became accustomed to doing naturally what Frimmer wanted.

Frimmer had realized a long time ago that anyone and everyone except James Frimmer II could be replaced. It was part of his Darwinian view of life and happiness. Loyalty and absolute obedience were crucial virtues needed to carry out Frimmer's business plans. Anything else would lead to inefficiencies and down a slippery slope to profits not maximized and riches not realized.

He could not abide by the sloth of unrealized profits and showed no restraint in getting his way. Frimmer was not averse to blackmail, kidnapping, assassination, or having a prosecutor in his pocket go after do-gooder judges, legislators or union leaders for no good reason at all. He had judges willing to rule in his favor to deal with do-gooder prosecutors. He had judges and prosecutors eliminated on a "market-inefficient" basis for not being willing to act in his favor. This tactic tended to have a profound impact on remaining judges and prosecutors who valued their liberty to live. Frimmer wasn't averse to ordering the "elimination of inefficient market elements" of any do-gooders who stood in his way. Sometimes it was for just cause and sometimes not. He wanted to make sure that people knew he wasn't called "Big Stake" for nothing, even if he considered the tag more legend than real and at first had hated it.

The best part about Frimmer's Law of Business Expansion is that the politicians had no idea they were on his team. Frimmer was at least four layers removed from the accountability and protected by dozens of fake special interest lobbying groups and political action slush fund committees with patriotic sounding names like Real Americans for One Percent Prosperity, Smart Dirty Energy for Freedom, and Business Leaders for Government Elimination.

"Pa, you were quite right. Democracy is a whore because it c
bought so cheaply," Frimmer said to the massive portrait of his father,
the long dead but never forgotten James Frimmer I. For decades, his father had fought do-gooder liberal politicians, the IRS, union organizers,
and environmental activists. Frimmer I hated human rights activists who
interrupted a profitable revival of industrial slavery in the early 1960s
and the FBI, which investigated black market profiteering during World
War II and the Vietnam War. Frimmer I had established the template of
Frimmer Empire Enterprises and Frimmer II took the family business
to the next level. Frimmer II believed it was the pioneering work of his
father that set the stage for the Real America revival.

"If you don't like what the government is doing, stop complaining.
Don't be a jackass and waste your time voting or talking about voting.
Just buy the damn thing," Frimmer the elder had told his youngest son.

For almost four decades, Frimmer had taken his father's advice to heart
and put it to work to protect the billions FEE had made in mining, oil
and natural gas extraction and refinement; financial speculation and energy market manipulation; prostitution, arms trafficking, identity theft,
credit card and insurance scams; banking, mortgage securitization and
foreclosure services; toxic dumping for profit, drug running and mercenary security services. One of Frimmer's pet entrepreneurial projects,
the FEE All-Services Assassination Bureau, was so highly regarded that
the security agencies for 28 countries, including the CIA, regularly contracted for its services. It was a Frimmer trait to provide supply for both
sides of the demand market and legality was but a minor technicality.

The prodigal bastard son

Before Frimmer II disappeared from public in the early 1980s, some of
the general facts of his life were known. He was a bastard son from the
only mistress Frimmer I ever had – a smart and tenacious 20th Century

frontier woman who ran a farm and ranch in South Dakota and didn't need a man or Frimmer I's money when he wanted her land for oil exploration. When four representatives from Frimmer Enterprises could not persuade Milly Johnson to sell, Frimmer I went himself. He eventually negotiated a futures contract and began a 20-year relationship with the high-spirited, no-nonsense Milly who bore him a precocious son. Thom Johnson worshipped his father and Frimmer I doted on his bastard son. He had taken a liking to the energetic and fearless boy who shined when compared to the lackluster output of his two non-bastard sons. "The slackers," Frimmer I called them and he was disgusted they were more interested in spending his money on art museums and running nonprofit foundations than doing the hard work of making money.

With his father's blessing, young Thom had his name changed to James Frimmer II when he was 10. Wrestling was the only sport he was interested in and he became good at it because he savored the one-on-one combat nature of the encounters. Frimmer II disavowed all other teenage social activities and decided early on he would be a successful businessman, which he considered "the highest righteous calling on earth." With his mother's blessing, he started his own produce delivery business at 12, even before he could legally drive. By the time he was 25 and a freshly minted MBA from the James Frimmer School of Business at Texas Grand Liberty University, he had pushed aside or destroyed his two half-brothers vying for the family crown.

"I know my bastard half-brother will be even more ruthless than my daddy and that's saying a lot," said art collector Daniel Frimmer to a reporter writing about Frimmer II's seizure of the family business. "He drove a big stake through me and he'll do it to anyone else who stands in his way." Frimmer II wasn't pleased that his half-brother had talked to the press and was annoyed that he ended up with the "big stake" nickname. He didn't like the publicity or the way the story correctly portrayed him. Frimmer II had promised his daddy that he wouldn't kill his half-brothers if they got in his way, but there was a loophole and Frimmer II was always good at finding loopholes – Papa Frimmer said nothing about killing the families of his half-brothers.

Daniel Frimmer was given $50 million, exiled to a quiet life in Monte Carlo and given simple instructions: keep your mouth shut or else I will kill your mother, your wife and three children. For the rest of his well-financed life, Daniel Frimmer never said a discouraging word about his half-brother. David Frimmer, the other half-brother, got the hint and was silenced at a cut-rate discount of $15 million.

Alas, the reporter who wrote the "Big Stake" story was not so lucky. He was kidnapped from a supermarket parking lot in New Jersey and flown to Texas on one of Frimmer's private jets. The reporter had to dig his grave on land Frimmer owned in a remote stretch of West Texas. His interrogation was taped and he was shot. It was the first of many Frimmer II opponent graves located in the tranquil setting that Frimmer named Happy Meadows.

Yes, Frimmer had taken his pa's advice and played the slow but ruthless long game to get what he wanted. Each day he strived to delegitimize government at all levels one step at a time. It was an efficient market-based approach to making sure the he maximized his riches by having local, state and federal governments do their best to serve his ends. Before the change to RAC, one of his budget wizards figured out that for every $1 million that he invested in politicians, government officials, reporters, and judges willing to do his bidding, he got back $35.675 million in profits.

With the formation of the Execution Channel under way, Frimmer was concerned about control. He assessed that his people could keep Bowie under control without much trouble but Jason Bravtart was another matter. Frimmer liked the young man's drive and vision, but there was something he didn't trust and Frimmer wasn't sure what it was. "I think we should keep an eye on young Bravtart," Frimmer said to Gunner. "He's got dreams of glory and can't turn off that public relations spigot of a mouth and I think he's drinking too much of that nutty Galtian cool aid. I like the kid, but he may not fit into our long-range plans."

"Yes, sir," Gunner said. It was a Tuesday and Gunner was dressed in a security uniform that showed him to be a colonel in Frimmer's private militia of more than 2,500 executives, mercenaries and financial alchemists. If you worked at the Dallas headquarters you got a rank and a uniform and Tuesday was mandatory battle fatigues day. Gunner said he would set up a comprehensive surveillance package on Bravtart and his wife by Mr. Jones, their top security contractor in California.

Frimmer did not wear a uniform and didn't want to be called a general. He didn't mind however when his immediate staff called him 'The Prince' when he wasn't around. Frimmer was as short as Napoleon but he preferred to be thought of as a Medici, a builder of modern corpo-nations.

The count

"What's the count today, Gun?" Frimmer asked his top aide, who often seemed to be attached to Frimmer's hip. The count was a throwback to the old days of Jimmy Frimmer I who used a collection of poker chips to keep track of those he had in his proverbial pocket. Frimmer the younger had upped the ante considerably since his father's day. Even he was amazed at times at the sheer number and occupational types of the people he kept on his payroll. He needed a staff of 24 alone to keep track of the politicians, bureaucrats, reporter and pundit shill publishers, judges, school teachers, intelligence operators, bloggers, paparazzi, televinet executives and producers, professional athletes, computer hackers and programmers, televinet news anchors, lifeguards, corrupt investors and financial advisors, regulators, realtors, musicians, actors, house cleaners, video game players, statisticians, local and state police officers, school bus drivers, landscape workers, prison guards and parole officers, nannies, bankers, thrift shop owners, toxic waste dumpers and body disposers.

The great news from Frimmer's perspective is that the per-unit price was dropping as the informant and active agent payroll grew. There was a high political demand to be on the payroll and, theoretically, in the good graces of those bankrolling the payroll. Frimmer was in his early 60s, still worked a minimum of 75 hours a week and felt that his best and most productive years were ahead of him. Each day he drank a specially made, highly potent kale concoction blender drink that was supposed to enhance his potency as a man, extend his life expectancy while pushing back the biological clock. Frimmer was determined to not to leave this vale of tears like his father who wallowed in dementia for far too long before his death.

"It's 4,123,585 as of 8 a.m. Dallas Standard Time today, sir," Gunner said as he has looked at the nationwide totals from a spreadsheet on his handheld compcom. Frimmer didn't keep poker chips as his father did, but he did have a personally-minted, gold coin collection on the immense 50-foot high wall opposite the window on the top floor of his penthouse office suite. Each day, a militia private came in and added or subtracted from the gold $50 coin count and used a specially made lift to go up and down. The count board alone was worth more than $200 million. Frimmer technically broke the law by keeping the dollar coins, but he didn't care because he had created and benefited from the RAC conversion and figured no one would screw with his right to keep whatever currency he wanted.

As he pondered which of two staff concubines he would fuck during a 15-minute break in the next few hours, Frimmer was puzzled by the count. "We didn't have much of a bump in the past week, did we?" It was true. The count was only up by 36 newly purchased pawns from the week before but Gunner, as always, checked his spreadsheet. "We are up some but we've had 62 natural deaths, 14 sanctioned terminations on personal treason charges and 33 suspects have been brought in for questioning after they dropped below the loyalty baseline," he said. "All in all, sir, I think it's been a positive week."

Frimmer nodded. He hated stupidity, do-gooders and disloyalty above all. He paid exceptionally well for people to do what he expected and he expected them to commit to doing exceptionally well for him 24 hours a day, seven days a week. The number of suspects on his payroll being brought in for questioning under new corporate intelligence guidelines passed in Congress was a potentially troubling number. Frimmer's self-proclaimed gift was that he often thought in geometric progressions. "Life is a pandemic waiting to happen," Frimmer once said at a board meeting for Frimmer Empire Enterprises. He didn't mean disease as much as subtle but potentially damaging variations in herd thinking among the Real American people.

"Do you think we should tighten up that loyalty baseline metric?" he asked, though he knew the question was more of a command.

"Good idea sir. The evidence is quite clear on the terminations that there were loyalty breach metrics broken but our interrogators are reporting that at least three-quarter of the suspects brought in for questioning were clearly non-threatening," Gunner said. "Given how saturated the currt weapons market is, I think anyone on your IP who buys from a competitor maybe is not a red level loyalty breach."

"Nobody is non-threatening. They just haven't been exposed yet," Frimmer countered. This reminded him that Gunner was up for his loyalty examination in the next month. Because Gunner was more important and knew more secrets, the next loyalty exam would be more thorough by Frimmer's counterintelligence bureau and would include a scientifically applied amount of torture not utilized in his previous loyalty exams.

It would be a shame if Gunner fell to the same fate as the past two chiefs of staff who had been released from further duty, extensively tortured to find out if they had talked at all (they hadn't), executed, and buried beneath the west Texas desert at Happy Meadows. Then their identities were wiped clean except for a few whispered rumors which served Frimmer well. It was a most efficient, if sometimes controversial, way of doing business and enhancing productivity. He had actually become somewhat fond of and informal with Gunner who had proven very efficient and talented during his 18 months at Frimmer's side. Gunner also knew many secrets, including the recent elimination of two foreign intelligence agents who had penetrated too far into the world's largest money laundering scheme.

But the biggest secret Gunner knew was not about business. Frimmer had a son named Thom Johnson. The 12-year-old boy lived in palatial splendor in Hong Kong and was cared for by his mother, a stunningly beautiful and highly trained courtesan of mixed Asiatic and Nordic stock who Frimmer had optioned for $2 million a year for the past 14 years. It was money well spent as Thom was home schooled by the fin-

taught the boy real world skills of martial arts, human the importance of all thing Frimmer.

Thom was also mentored by a philosophical master in the hidden arts of "Metaphysico-theologo-cosmonigology," a resurrected and reshaped 18th-century ethos that explained the mysterious driving force of the universe, namely capitalism with no boundaries and no restraint. Frimmer wanted to train his son right and prepare him to be heir apparent. But his main goal now was training and to protect Thom from the chaos of the Real American cycle of economic destruction and bloodthirsty competitors who would kidnap him to put Frimmer at a competitive disadvantage. Frimmer hoped the conglomerate he had built would be renamed Johnson Empire Enterprise in homage to his mother and he was determined that Thom would be a general ready to assume his post when the time was right.

Thom had yet to meet his father, but had been told he was an important, money-making player in the universe. Thom thought that perhaps his father was even a true living God but he did not know his name. Frimmer planned to keep it that way for another eight years. Frimmer had mapped out a schedule for coming out from behind the curtain of secrecy and to show the world that he did exist and the legend could then merge with a real man. His son would be ready to follow in his footsteps, like Alexander the Great.

Defining the Galtian Imperatives

Frimmer bankrolled seven research institutes that churned out study after study and five media companies that churned out story after story dedicated to the premise that what was good for conglomerations like Frimmer Empire Enterprises was good for Real America and thereby strengthened the Galtian Imperatives. Frimmer took advantage of a quirk in the evolution of the Galtian Imperatives because no what they were but an overwhelmingly majority of Real Americans loved the fact that they existed. Frimmer made it one of his top communication priorities to control the shifting meanings, prophecies, and natural law interpretations of the Galtian Imperatives. This led to widespread acceptance of vital economic truths that few understood but all accepted without much reflection or investigation.

Frimmer was particularly pleased with a study from his Job Creating Institute that used no definable research but concluded without a doubt that a tax-free environment led to higher levels of self-esteem and confidence among the "Guardians of Galt" and the job-creating classes.

"If the top levels of money makers are feeling optimistic, it leads to higher levels of confidence in the overall economy," the study said. The findings of the study titled "Why Coddling the Maker Class is a Galtian Imperative" immediately became accepted free market gospel and was hailed as groundbreaking by one Galtian expert. "This study doesn't insult readers with analysis and evidence but makes a convincing intuitive case that the psychological well-being of our job-creating heroes is a top Galtian Imperative. Their well-being must be nurtured and never taken for granted," said Frank Major in a column for Real American Digest of Economic Affairs, a Frimmer-funded publication from another Frimmer-funded think tank. "Our Guardians of Galt need lower taxes and austerity to pave the way for their investing and producing prowess to combat the moral depravity of the moocher classes."

Just before the launch of the Execution Channel, Frimmer had Bowie give an important speech at the Frimmer-funded Institute for Complete Tax Elimination and Business Advocacy in Houston, the new capital of the also Frimmer-backed New Southern Alliance. Bowie made the case for increasing new business judicial powers and he called on Real

Americans to reject the idea of good governance because it was a costly detour on the road to getting rid of government altogether.

"We are building an infrastructure of sound morals and true economics in fidelity to our glorious Galtian Imperatives. Good government cannot be allowed to exist because it is a bite of the poisonous apple. Sound government is a dangerous principle we oppose at every level. This treachery threatens freedom-loving Real Americans because it invites tyranny in through the back door with promises of equal opportunity and justice for all. We cannot have justice for all but we can embrace the Galtian Imperatives. These tell us that corporations are not only people but our friends and loved ones that have our best interests at heart. The same cannot be said for so-called good government, which deceives us and leads to job-killing taxes and costly programs which do little but encourage more looting, taking and mooching." The staff at the Institute for Complete Tax Elimination and Business Advocacy had written the Bowie's speech to bolster a new initiative: to make personal and media criticism of corporations a felony in the Real American Republic of Texas and six other RAP-dominated states Frimmer controlled.

Frimmer took the long view on certain matters and often took counter-intuitive actions that other so-called political experts would have called bad investments. For example, when Frimmer was advised that certain candidates he backed had no chance of winning, mostly in states he didn't control, he doubled down on financial support and organization help from his think tanks and public relations hit squads. Even if that race turned out to be a loser, Frimmer figured the losing candidate would be grateful for the strong support in a losing cause and would become a loyal worker bee for Frimmer. The winning do-gooder would expend so much money to win and energy to fight back against the onslaught of false accusations from Frimmer's political hit squads that they would be fearful of doing much legislatively to weaken their re-election chances. For Frimmer it was a win-win result that would pay off in the long run.

In one of his most strategic of gambits, he joined the anti-abortion fight at the beginning of the decade not because he cared about the issue – rather he cared about the power he could exert by being on the right side of the issue with mostly male lawmakers in many important states. Through his research organizations and political action committees that left not a trace of his handiwork, Frimmer backed efforts to restrict abortion to within five hours of conception. When those same lawmakers then moved further to restrict and outlaw women's contraceptive and health-care services, Frimmer didn't mind and in fact saw a winning business opportunity through his black market pharmaceutical shops and back alley abortion clinics.

Before the newly constituted Liberty Court could hear a case and outlaw abortion once and for all, Frimmer decided it was time to put a lid on the issue and strike a blow for state's rights. His operatives had Bowie make a major, nationally televised speech telling the country there was no time to wait and action was needed to save "our great Republic of Texas and Real America from falling into the pits of doom." Bowie was happy to make headlines and satisfy his religious militia base with a grand historical measure.

Bowie didn't disappoint Frimmer. He not only outlawed abortion by emergency decree but made it a capital offense for both the doctor and patient. Speaking at the 2017 Real American Party: Revolution Forever Convention, Bowie drew boisterous cheers when he said "no compromise, no quarter" could be allowed when it came to defining the primacy of sperm. "My fellow Real Americans, we cannot discriminate against sperm or devalue how it arrives to that special place of conception. Just because we don't provide health care for them while they are in the womb or care for them after they are born, we are not without compassion for innocent fetuses when they snuggle in the womb. We treasure these unborn children as a powerful political tool to keep wayward, slutty women in their place. There can be no exceptions. We can't allow sideshow issues like rape or incest or concern about the mother's health stop us from enforcing our unquestioned virtue."

Harnessing the Galtian Wave

When Galt mania emerged as a serious political force, Frimmer had been briefed about Randian outlines and the popular deity known as John Galt. He couldn't fully comprehend the fascination or devotion over fictional characters and the monomaniacal writer who created them, but he did appreciate their strong value as propaganda for a new age of corporate domination in which large monopolies would slug it out for prominence and market share. He bought hundreds of thousands of copies of *Atlas Shrugged* and had them distributed to his rank and file and those on his influence payroll. They were instructed to respect the power of selfishness that drove makers and jobs creators to create prosperity. Frimmer wanted them to believe, or at least understand, that he, a maker and job creator extraordinaire, was in charge and they owed their existence in the emerging social order to him.

One of Frimmer's think tanks copied and then refined the concept of no fuss lawmaking with the formation of the Real American Easy to Pass Law Council. The goal was to provide legislation-by-the-numbers templates for laws that would benefit Frimmer even if the states didn't need the laws.

"They don't have to think anymore. We do the thinking for them. We just cut and paste our template into their bills and off they go to the races. When we did a test run in New Hampshire a few years ago, the Mad

Hatters there proved they didn't even have to bother with hearings because we supply our canned research to save them time and money. These New Hampshire Mad Hatters were given talking points and we found that when they said 'four legs good, two legs bad' again and again, the media sycophants and opponents simply succumbed to exhaustion. Our lawmakers get a chance to prove they are on the right side of the new history and don't have to exert much effort in the process," Gunner said to Frimmer.

The RAEPLC playbook was refined year after year and in Bowie they had a willing partner to extol its virtues. Bowie made more national and global headlines when he decisively and brilliantly solved the state's public pension problem by having it declared insolvent and seizing the 138.5 billion RAC pension portfolio as forfeiture. "This pension scheme was a vast criminal enterprise that taxpayers were forced to take part in, my fellow patriots. We will direct half to pay for private militias and the rest as a rebate to the top one percent of taxpayers," Bowie said after calling out the RART Militia under his control and enforcing a curfew when many Texans didn't take kindly to his proposal. "These Guardians of Galt will invest this money wisely to create jobs and prosperity for all."

By emergency executive order, Bowie then eliminated the final remnants of public and private sector unions by declaring them "un-Real American and contrary to the requirements of Galtian Imperatives." When his opponents sued him, he remade the court system by emergency executive order "to protect Real Americans from frivolous lawsuits."

Bowie further solidified his national stature when he did what many RAP political leaders only dreamed of and started the process of dismantling the RART public school system. He vowed by that by 2020, there would be no more public schools. Parents would then be freed from the tyranny of a system that could no longer be economically justified.

etting a standard for Real America and even the world to admire," Bowie said in a speech before the RART legislature. "When the cost-efficient choice of good ole' home schooling is an option, especially now that so many unemployed parents are home, we can't ask taxpayers to continue to pay for a corrupt and outdated system that has nothing to do with education but everything to do with a lifetime employment scheme for teachers who don't embrace our Real American values. It's time we fully solve the problem once and for all with home schooling and for-profit schools that will teach our children proper lessons about the Galtian Imperatives. Public education costs us money that could be better spent, and this new wave of innovation will be more economically efficient. Think of how quickly we will create new generations of ill-educated workers who will be happy to take low-wage jobs and never ask questions."

Frimmer was impressed and he was not alone. "With partners like Gov. Bowie, we are closer to making the Galtian Imperatives the life-blood of our economy and culture. We are proud to have written the template for this type of new democracy in which much is accomplished but exactly what is accomplished is never known," said Abram Jachoof, president and CEO of the Real American Easy to Pass Law Council.

The FEE machine was all going well, almost too well. The more Frimmer pondered the potential of the Execution Channel concept, the more he tallied up the coming financial and political benefits. Frimmer was a disciplined investor and manipulator and rarely counted profits before they arrived. But he had an intuition that the Execution Channel would be big, very big, and it could vault him into the top economic power spot in a splintered country. He felt his pa's spirit and imagined the old man saying his bastard son was the one to solidify the Frimmer legacy.

Frimmer II knew he was the right man in the right place with the right opportunity to seize it all. He would become The Prince.

Frimmer could not have foreseen the true fragility of his grip on power. It was a lesson he would learn the hard way, courtesy of a popular psychic by the name of Penelope who resided in the SoCal Liberty Territory.

CHAPTER SEVEN
SPIRITS IN THE NIGHT

"History has no function in America except to divide people and piss them off to no end."

– PENELOPE THE PSYCHIC

D espite her husband's skepticism, Sandy Bravtart sang the praises of Penelope the Psychic to her circle of friends and work colleagues. "Penelope gets it. She understands the universe and she gets me," she told one and all. Jason loved his wife dearly and he decided to give Penelope the benefit of the doubt, especially after her prophecy about The Execution Channel came true. This was good news for Penelope because it led Sandy to talk often about Jason. When Sandy talked to Penelope about Jason, Penelope listened carefully. Jason, after all, was one of the people she was paid to inform on.

In a time when everything seemed a little extraordinary, Penelope ran a remarkable business in Venice Beach. Penelope was no typical fake medium, psychic, astrologer or confidante to so many troubled souls. She had many talents and prided herself on being a well-rounded entrepreneur, con artist, a spy for the British and German secret services, and a well-paid double-agent informant for five militia groups. Penelope didn't ask for the role but she became the deus ex machina, a plot twist from the gods that altered the destiny of The Execution Channel.

It has not been an easy road for Penelope and informing for the militias was not a choice as we will see later in this tale. She had avoided political entanglements since her arrival in California in early 2015 and paid her local militia protection fees on time and in full each month. She had kept up good relations with the up and coming militia units which had taken most over most public sector functions in the newly-named SoCal

Liberty Territory. Penelope wanted to keep that low profile until her client Sandy Bravtart surprised her with a favor she didn't want. When Penelope got a request for an interview from a militia media site overseen by Sandy, she could not turn it down.

"I provide a service between consenting adults," she said coyly to the young televinet reporter named Sam who worked as a propaganda specialist for Sandy Bravtart at the 1st John Galt SoCal Militia. The reporter was working a story about a boom in psychic and alternative religion outlets to meet a demand in high anxiety, a result many said of the Galtian Revolution sweeping throughout Real America.

"We live in a glorious but anxious age of a Real America rebirth. We have the Galtian Imperatives which guide us but we all seek assurance and answers not readily available in books or on the televinet," Penelope said to Sam. She wanted to bed him but thought better of it given the surveillance she suspected she was under. She also didn't want or need a lovesick militia groupie hanging around like a baby puppy always peeing excitedly on the floor. But she figured a militia-sanctioned story would be good for business so she flirted some with the aspiring reporter and set the parameters of the story on I Ching coins, the proper reading of tarot cards, séances and recent developments in Galtian astrological charts. When the reporter started asking questions about her "alleged mysterious past," she laughed and leaned over for him to get a lengthy look at her at her braless breasts.

After an awkward moment or two of silence by Sam, she gently took control by asking questions about his militia experiences and thoughts about Real American history. Penelope ran out the clock on the interview and sent Sam on his way and resumed her schedule, which included sessions with agents from German and British secret services.

Her regularly scheduled session with Robert from MI-6 was a bi-weekly update on military and political operations being planned by Real American militias in SoCal. Penelope had heard rumors that the California civil war might break out soon. The state had already split into two sectors, one mostly north, which rejected the Galtian Imperatives, and pro-Galtian Imperatives territory in the south. Penelope had heard from one talkative militia officer that ground zero of the likely conflict was the fertile Central Valley region.

"We had these loony Yanks pegged right in 1775. It took about 250 years but we figured sooner or later they were going to really crack up. This is making 1861 look like a picnic, but the problem is that they are dragging the rest of the world down," said Roger of MI-6 whose name of course wasn't really Roger. He worked as an IT consultant for a multinational corporation that was helping militia units throughout the country build their IT networks. It was a solid cover, he insisted. Penelope noticed he liked to pepper his conversations with grand historical references and metaphors.

"The militia gangs are brawling in the streets and they are armed to the teeth, determined to prove that their militia has the most devotion to Galt, free markets and liberty. Christ, the chaos and killings are like your Munich in the late 1920s. Their public shootouts seem to have no purpose except to prove they can have them. They are a particularly ignorant lot and their gift is to practice nihilism of the highest order. We are concerned that they will finally tank the world economy for good but my job is to make sure one of the militia nuts doesn't get control of a loose nuke or two and hasten the end of days and the rest of us."

Penelope sighed as Roger babbled on and on. He was annoying, but paid his stipends to her Australian bank account on time and he was right. America as a country, an idea, and an ideal was falling apart as quickly as the federal government. She sensed her days in SoCal were coming to an end. During most of the more than two decades she lived in America, first as a dutiful wife of an American and then on the run as a card shark and grifter, Penelope had paid hardly any attention to political developments or what she had considered the "silly" Red/Blue state divide that so many political types endlessly talked about. But since resurfacing with a new name, vocation and Venice Beach location, remaining blissfully ignorant was no longer an option.

States' rights, unfettered personal liberty and the gleeful demise of a federal government represented the passions of the day for a healthy portion of the country. All in all, this was good for Penelope's business. Massive change prompted massive anxiety and this equated to plenty of anxious people seeking assurance, seeking answers, and seeking some semblance of comfort in a world gone chaotic. An onset of mass political paranoia was even better but Penelope knew that there was a cost to be paid for the anarchy.

She had seen her home country of East Germany fall apart in the seeming blink of an eye almost three decades before and it left an impression on her. "History doesn't give a fuck about anyone," she wrote in a secret diary that later became the international best seller about her travels and adventures in Real America. "History has no function in America except to divide people and piss them off to no end."

Informing made her feel right at home. It was much more profitable and preferable now than when she had been an informant growing up in East Germany for the notorious secret service agency Stasi. "One never knows what experiences in life will prove immensely helpful," she said to Stefan her current German secret service handler who himself was a Stasi veteran and a well-paid double agent as an undercover consultant to two Arizona militias. The Arizona militia leaders, known as a particularly lethal bunch of former motorcycle club outlaws, trusted Stefan owing to his pure Aryan bloodlines and wanted him on board when the race war they wanted to happen would in fact happen.

Penelope opened Penelope's Place in early 2015 between a surfing equipment store on side and a militia weapons bazaar on the other side. She began to attract clients connected to the dwindling entertainment industry, financial speculators and, surprisingly to her, a number of up-and-comers in Real American militia units. She was happy to supply empathy and an ability to listen without judgment. She also quickly picked up on the language and fads of Real America and developed a particular talent for channeling Ayn Rand and Dagny Taggart, the reigning free-market deities of the new economic era. She was also a savvy marketer and had a digital sign on the wall of her drawing room with a quote from the famous speech from *Atlas Shrugged* that John Galt made to the country:

"With the sign of the dollar as our symbol – the sign of free trade and
free minds – we will move to reclaim this country once more
from the important savages who never discovered
its nature, its meaning, its splendor."

More than one militia member was brought to tears when reading the sign and understanding its potency.

Her sitting room was filled with the constant, quiet sound of barely touching wind chimes and gypsy colors of red and black. Penelope dressed the part in lace and silk with a rainbow-colored headband across her long blonde hair that disguised her real age by more than a decade. She looked more like a beautifully aging Hollywood starlet than a middle-aged woman with plenty to hide.

A legacy of con

This was one of her best and safest cons of her life and even Penelope sometimes forgot the boundaries of the con and herself. Penelope the Psychic to the stars, financial wizards and militia leaders was actually her third incarnation, though it could have been her fourth depending on how it was categorized. Penelope herself sometimes lost count. Penelope was born Gretta Brecht in the former East Germany the year the Berlin Wall went up. That she had been a Stasi informer for seven years was no surprise given that an estimated 83 percent of the population in East Germany had been an informer at one time or another in their adult lives.

Gretta did just enough informing for the Stasi to be considered a trustworthy snitch whose product was otherwise unremarkable. It was part of her motto of doing just enough to remain invisible in sight. She worked as the executive secretary for a machine parts export company, taught herself English and had an economically advantageous affair with her boss. She moved up in the world when she developed skills as an effective embezzler.

At first it was 20 East German marks for a decent lunch, then 50 marks for a pedicure and hairdressing trip, 400 marks for black market blue jeans and Beatles' records and then it was 50,000 marks. Gretta discovered how resourceful she could be. Though the East German Mark was a worthless currency outside of East Germany, Gretta figured out a black market way to convert goods, services and East German marks into West German marks which a West German cousin then converted into dollars and deposited into a bank in Berlin. At the peak of her embezzling, she managed to save $50,000 in the secret account. Later in the early 1990s, after the Berlin Wall fell and German reunification took place, Gretta had hoped that the economic chaos would provide excellent cover for her thefts.

There was an initial interview after a financial investigation audit turned up "serious financial irregularities" but, much to her shock, the focus wasn't on her. For the first and not the last time, she was lucky – her boss had been embezzling even greater amounts of factory money, in part to pay bribes to Communist Party officials so he and his family could travel outside the country. Gretta was thankful for the reprieve and, before proper charges could be filed against anyone, she destroyed as much of the incriminating paperwork as possible and found a human escape hatch. She met, quickly seduced and married an American toy salesman named Jake MacDonald from Ohio who had been sent to Berlin to set up a new distribution network. "I had him the second I started sucking his cock," she recounted in her book, *Surviving the Real America Crack Up*.

Following their return to America, Gretta discovered she was wife to a dullard, "the most boring man ever conceived," she said in her book. Jake was, if nothing else, predictable. He worked 62.5 hours a week as a senior sales executive at American Toy & Games and within each of those working weeks he expected two quick fucks, one blow job and at least three home-cooked meals. Despite years of trying, the couple could not conceive a child, which Gretta later realized was a gift from heaven.

Jake's sole inspiration was sports in general and the football Cleveland Browns in particular. Gretta had dealt with sports-obsessed men in Germany and had never grasped the fascination for grown men following grown men getting paid good money to play games. When the Brown's franchise moved to Baltimore in 1996, Jake succumbed to a lengthy depression that only lifted when a new franchise arrived a few years later.

Gretta dared to go existential on Jake one Sunday by asking "Does football really matter?" as he prepared to sit down for hours of football immersion. Jake reacted as if she had questioned the gravitational pull in the solar system. He told her she was a "fucking moron" and slammed the door on his way out to a local bar. When they took a spring trip to New York, Gretta was appalled to spend almost the entire the visit by herself while Jake attended something called the NFL draft for new players.

During her alone time in New York, Gretta stopped by a psychic named Penelope who had a small salon in Greenwich Village. When Penelope promised Gretta adventure and romance, she yearned to believe but realized it was not going to be with Jake. While sitting in a bar nursing a whiskey, she looked up at a television and was stunned to see her husband dressed like a dog at the NFL draft. He was jumping up and down and she thought he was barking. After 10 years, she decided a return to her deadly dull life in the Cleveland suburb of Parma Heights was not in her best interests.

Gretta MacDonald found another escape hatch and rekindled her true callings as a con artist and thief when she fell quickly for a small-time con man running an auto insurance scam ring. She easily saw through the ploy of Tito Roberts but was thrilled by his audacity. It was an alternative to her uninspiring life of a loan originating officer in a boring bank and being married to a dullard.

Within days she left the world of Jake behind and hit the road with Tito to begin her next career as a grifter. Tito was 10 years younger than she was and like Gretta, he had been strictly small time. But Gretta had ambitions, even a guiding philosophy. During all those years with Jake, she developed a fantasy defense mechanism. She treated her life as an ongoing movie and strived to manipulate people and situations with the skill of a screenwriter. She imagined starring in a romantic adventure thriller of her own creation and playing a criminal was far more creative and exciting than playing it safe and easy. She practiced lines she wrote for herself and made sure she hit her stage marks. She taught herself to think ahead like a chess master and to know at all times the location of the quickest exit door.

Through a network of former contacts, she tracked down and then seduced a former East German Stasi agent in Chicago named Luda who had been her handler for a while back in the 1980s. Luda had remade himself as a corporate espionage expert, but his true genius was as one of the top document forgers in the world and he could create a highly layered and detailed legend for almost anyone. He created two sets of new identities and legends and cautioned her to use them carefully. The first was the name of Lolita McShay, a small town bank employee from Vermont who had a widowed mother in Philadelphia.

Lolita and Tito began working small but effective mistress blackmail traps against middle-aged corporate executives and prominent legislators in four states. Tito helped by providing the threat of bodily harm to those who could not bring themselves to pay for the photos, videos and accompanying documentation.

Along the way, Lolita met a lonely University of Chicago mathematics professor named Robert Levster who taught her how to play poker and cheat at blackjack in casinos by counting cards. She became fascinated by cards, reading all the books she could get her hands on. At Levster's urging, she became his best student and nurtured her talent wisely by not winning too much in one sitting and by slipping in and before attracting too much security attention.

Lolita also discovered she could play poker at the professional level, which was timely given the growth of professional poker tournaments and amateurs seeking to strike it rich playing Texas Hold 'Em. She was hooked and after a few years she dumped Tito, who really was a small-time bore. She began working the competitive and underground poker circuits across the nation.

She was an expert reader of the table and could detect even the slightest of tells in the best of players. She was also sufficiently paranoid and played it smart by keeping a low profile through the first years of online tournaments and never playing in a televised tourney. It was her German discipline that pushed her to never give into cleaning out a particular game or charity poker event. Lolita was banking money in several overseas accounts, always ready to drop her identity and disappear if necessary. She estimated that $1,000 to $2,000 a day was a good payday compared to the meager existence she had in East Germany.

Lolita was disciplined until, like all mortals, she wasn't. In 2005, she met and fell for a con man who dealt in the new profitable frontier of mortgage securities. Mark Depart had worked in boiler rooms selling bogus stocks for a few decades and had made a small fortune. Then the real estate boom in the first decade of the 21st century made everyone delirious.

"This is the easiest money ever. There are no regulations and even if there were, there are no regulators to do anything about it. It's the greatest con ever," Depart said to Lolita in bed the night they met at a private poker game in San Diego. Depart and Lolita teamed up to create more than 5,200 fraudulent mortgage loan applications through a sham ɯortgage business named PickItRight Loan. They targeted low income people, including the unemployed, the homeless and those who didn't exist except on paper. There was little chance that more than 2 percent of the loans could ever be repaid – in part because 98 percent of the loans were fakes – but that didn't matter to PickItRight. Depart turned around and sold the loans to a Frimmer-owned securitization company. Those loans were then bundled and resold again to a wide range of private and institutional investors. "Eventually, someone is going to be left holding the bag but it won't be us," Depart said as he and Lolita pocketed nearly $6.5 million in assorted fees before declaring bankruptcy and closing up shop in early 2007.

The day after putting the closed sign on the door, Depart disappeared without a trace, even though they had made plans to bolt together. She had only made $55,000 and it was her signature and fantasy entries on almost all the loan documents representing PickItRight. Depart had flown the coop just before the federal regulators and the FBI started snooping around. Depart had thoughtfully left Lolita stuck with a lease on their now closed office and tens of thousands of dollars in unpaid vendor bills. "I fell for a con," she said to a homeless man on a park bench in San Diego. She was determined never to make that mistake again.

So long Lolita

She wasted no time in getting as far away from San Diego as possible. She figured the authorities had her name but otherwise she was still relatively unknown. She headed east to Atlantic City and New York and worked the East Coast casino and underground poker circuit for a few years. After a few years of setbacks – she lost one-half of her stash in the stock market crash of 2008 and paid out of pocket for breast cancer treatment – Lolita needed fiscal liquidity quickly and she hit the casinos in Atlantic City. Whether it was bad karma or bad judgment, she became sloppy and made mistakes which exposed her to the elements of fate.

Lolita was normally disciplined and had a system to keep it that way. But she took a risk when she pushed her winning method at the blackjack table. It had been a while since she had taken such a risk and while she was doing it, she swore it would be just this once. She felt she had played the role of a middle-aged, lucky working stiff well when she began walking away from the mid-level casino with $16,000. After she cashed in her chips, three plain clothes security guards surrounded her barely 10 steps away from the front door.

Lolita protested she had done nothing wrong and had simply got lucky while visiting her ailing mother in Philadelphia. "I'm an unemployed bank administrator," she said. Sid, the casino security chief, was impressed with the quality of her cheating but didn't buy her story. "I'm sure if we dig deep enough, we will find that your name isn't Lolita, your mother isn't ill and you aren't from Putney, Vermont," Sid said. "Frankly, I don't give a fuck who you are but I know what you do. You're a counter and a cheat and let me make myself perfectly clear."

Sid made himself perfectly clear by backhanding Lolita with a violent slap that propelled her out of the chair and onto the floor. Sid took the entire $16,000 in winnings and an extra $2,000 from her. "Consider it a service fee," he said. She was told she was persona non grata in Atlantic City and Las Vegas until "hell freezes over." Sid promised "the next reception won't be so delightful," if she didn't get the point. Lolita got the point.

After a few years working the underground poker circuit, Lolita heard from Luda that she had been indicted for fraud in connection with PickItRightLoan and the FBI was trying to track her down. One night, she was walking around Greenwich Village considering her next moves. The November chill dampened her spirits but also hardened her resolve. She needed a change of identity and venue and figured the timing couldn't be better. The economy had sunken further and the country seemed to her to be on the verge of some sort of civil war.

"The talk is crazy and getting crazier, like the patients have escaped and want to set up a country-wide asylum," a coffee shop waitress said to her a few weeks earlier while they watched the latest news about fist-fights on the floor of Congress and private militias taking over small towns and cities in a few Western states. Lolita did not have a university education, but the German DNA in her was terrified of anarchy because the cost was so high. In her experience, anarchy led to fascism, Hitler, inflation, extermination camps and genocide, war, Communism, concentration camps, fear and terror and secret police everywhere. None of it was good.

Near Washington Square, she saw the psychic shop she had visited years earlier. It was no longer called Penelope's Place but was named Enchantachant Psychic Services. "Where is Penelope?" she asked the receptionist named Pam, who was dressed as a junior corporate accountant.

"Funny, I get asked that question a few times a year. Penelope, the old lady, died a few years ago, I heard," said the receptionist. "I guess the company took this place over and it became the first store. We now have 17 salons in the Northeast and are looking to expand throughout the country, or at least the safe parts of what's left of the country. Are you interested in a franchise?"

Lolita declined the offer and walked around. She saw a small bar with complimentary wine, cheeses and crackers, Internet chair consoles, eyeglass-style vidgame devices, medical marijuana dispensary, and massage tables for clients waiting to see the six resident psychics. She thanked the receptionist and left to sit down at a nearby café and to ponder her next move. It didn't take long for her to come up with an answer that fit her new reality of dwindling bank accounts, a need for a new identity and, most of all, a career change to best utilize her talents. Within 24 hours on that fateful November day in the year of 2014 – when the Real American Party took control of eight state legislatures and saw 120 members elected to Congress and 15 to the Senate in mid-term elections – Lolita boarded a bus to California with the new identity of Cathy Delison and a plan to set up shop as Penelope the Psychic.

For more than two years she hid in plain sight until Mr. Jones discovered who she was.

CHAPTER EIGHT

AN UNWELCOME GUEST

"It's just great that people feel better when they have no jobs or they can't drink the water or breathe the air or send their kids to school as long as government has been put in its place. I think right-minded historians will look back and call this the dawn of a breakthrough epoch when liberty and free markets reigned supreme."

– MR. JONES

In the summer of 2017, a month after Sandy Bravtart shared the news with Penelope about Jason's vision for the Execution Channel, Penelope's hand-held compcam vibrated with a security prompter when her 10 a.m. appointment came through the door at 9:58. Penelope put down her third cup of coffee of the day and immediately sensed something slightly off. Sean Linson, a former Hollywood screenwriter now down on his luck and trying to escape from the SoCal Liberty Territory, was always two minutes late and that never varied. When Penelope stepped into her small waiting room, she saw it wasn't Linson.

She looked at the video feed on her compcam and saw nothing. She was confused and didn't know where this unfamiliar man had come from. He wore a khaki brown trench coat, a rare sight on Venice Beach, and if forced to describe him quickly she would have said "tall, dark and handsome." He was dressed smartly as a top corporate executive or a Gestapo agent from the movies. He wore a tailored pinstripe grey suit, light blue shirt and a paisley tie and his demeanor was strikingly distinct from her typical client. Penelope tried not to be too obvious but she looked again and saw he was strikingly handsome with a chiseled chin, slightly tanned face and neatly trimmed hair. He seemed a referral from Hollywood central casting, the kind easily embraced by cameras.

"Can I help you?" she said. For some reason, she noticed, the wind chimes had stopped their light but constant chiming.

"Yes, I'd like to get a reading and I've heard you're the best medium around," he said. "I need your assessment on how the stars are aligning for my future."

"I'm sorry sir, but I don't take walk-in appointments." She paused and focused her eyes on his bright blue eyes, which were equally focused on hers. "If you noticed my sign outdoors, it said by appointment only. And my 10 o'clock client will be here any second now."

"I think not," he said in a calm voice, the assuring type heard in friendly televinet public service commercials talking about the glories of the new Galtian age. "I think we can safely assume that Mr. Linson now resides in the ranks of former clients."

"Excuse me." She didn't like the sound of his voice and certainly didn't like the chilly stillness in his eyes. "I don't understand."

She looked at her compcam security camera feed again and was surprised to see two black security limousines were parked in front and surrounded by six security guards. He noticed her confusion. "I wouldn't worry about your security system. We cut into it for a brief time so you wouldn't be startled by new guests," he said.

She simply nodded.

"As for Mr. Linson, I don't think proper psychic readings will be a concern of his any longer."

'I am sorry, but you are not explaining yourself. Was Sean in an accident or hurt?"

"No, I would say nothing like that. At least yet," he said.

She decided to play semi-dumb. "I am sorry, Mr., ah, I did not get your name because you did not tell me. I am not comfortable with this puzzling conversation. If you would be so kind as to leave before I call the authorities."

"No, Penelope, you don't need to do that. I know what you pay for protection and the patriotic soldiers of the South Venice Beach Militia thank you for paying the correct amount and on time every month. Not everyone is so diligent." He paused. "You can call me Mr. Jones if you like."

Penelope wanted to close her eyes and take a meditation break to deal with this threat that had seemingly come from nowhere. But her eyes did not close and no calm would come. She rightly sensed danger.

"I still don't understand what this is about."

"We know that Linson and his wife Debbie were trying to get exit visas. I guess you could say they got their wish and are heading to a better place they tell me." Penelope wanted to ask who "they" were but thought better of it. She figured it was something militia related as everyone was on edge not to get on the wrong side of militia counterintelligence units operating in the SoCal region.

"Here's my take. The best-case scenario for them is that they have enough money for ransom to the militia group holding them. After a sizable payout and possibly a lengthy stay in a re-education camp, they could emerge as true rehabilitated citizens of Real America suitable for a reality televinet show."

Penelope nodded and thought of a popular televinet show *Embracing Galt,* which chronicled the return to normalcy of former Galtian non-believers and liberals who had spent time at re-education camps and now embraced the Galtian Imperatives. *Embracing Galt* captured the new way of living, of hating government and liberals, of loving militias and corporations who promised "prosperity for all," even if they only delivered prosperity for a few.

Mr. Jones continued, "The best-case two scenario is that they will take part in public show trials, confess their sins to the world, plead their fidelity to the Galtian Imperatives and either be executed or sent to a corporate work prison where, I've been told, few survive with their sanity or their health."

Mr. Jones paused for a second and Penelope averted her eyes slightly. His eye contact with her continued to make her anxious and it was hard to get a read. She couldn't determine his age. His dirty blonde, smartly gelled hair said early 40s, but his face and eyes and voice signaled the experience of one in their 60s.

"The worst-case scenarios are, well, truly worst case as I'm sure you can imagine," he continued. "I think if they are lucky, there will be quick trials before the ruling local militia. Hopefully for their sake, such a procedure will lead to quick executions, probably one shot each in the head, and if proper procedures are followed, their families will be charged for the bullets and the legal accommodations. Luckily, the families won't have to pay much for a burial because the militias practice market efficiency and most bodies these days are being dumped at sea for sharks to consume. This service is becoming quite the job-creating industry so it's win-win for a lot of people. Did you know we learned that little trick of disposing the evidence from our good and efficiently ruthless friends in in Chile and Argentina? They became experts at disappearing bodies in the 1970s. More importantly, they knew how to make a point."

"I see," she said. For months she had heard rumors of people disappearing completely as though they had vaporized into thin air or been sent to a different planet. She had thought the disappeared had just migrated

ꞮꞮꞮꞮꞮꞮ ꞮꞮ anti-Galtian sanctuaries or crossed the Mexican border and headed to safe émigré enclaves.

"This is a remarkable age we inhabit. From my perspective, and I admit it might be a limited one, the huge benefit from chaotic terror and anarchy like this is how quickly people fall into line, even more than before because you don't know – you don't know if your good acts or even good thoughts will get you anywhere or provide salvation. I think Lenin, Stalin, Hitler, and Mao were trailblazers with such policies of persuasion. Fear is a fine motivator and I can barely keep up with the number of clients who want our services because, well, they are afraid." Jones had emitted a small laugh that Penelope regarded as sinister.

Penelope realized that Mr. Jones was accustomed to speaking without interruption and she had no desire to break the flow. "The irony is almost too much to consider. For decades, these anti-government patriots preached fear and loathing and sure enough, it became a self-fulfilling prophecy. I always found it curious that people would howl if government wasted a nickel or forced them to pay for food safety or the roads they drove on but, and pardon my vulgarity, took it as point of pride to get fucked up the ass and ripped off excessively time and again by the private sector. I guess people feel better when they have no jobs or they can't drink the water or breathe the air or send their kids to school as long as government has been put in its place. I think right-minded historians will look back and call this the dawn of a breakthrough epoch when liberty and free markets reigned supreme. We are putting people back where they rightfully belong as servants of this glorious new age of prosperity. I call that progress, don't you?"

Penelope nodded not in agreement but more because his cold logic reminded her of growing up in East Germany when institutionalized fear was pervasive.

"So, to make a long story short, if Sean and Debbie aren't lucky in being tried and executed quickly, they could be interrogated for a long time, long beyond the time when any useful information could be extracted and that's if they are guilty of subversive behavior. It actually gets worse if they're innocent because alas, too many sadists have found a calling and don't like being denied."

"What are they being charged with?" was all Penelope could muster for a response.

"Charges? That is such an old-fashioned sensibility," he said. "I have no idea. Do you? I took a quick look at their file on my way here. He was a former journalist turned screenwriter turned failed novelist. She worked as a political consultant for liberally-tainted political candidates. What kind of productive lives are those? Maybe he pissed someone off a while ago and that someone held a grudge. Maybe he was behind on his protection payments or she didn't bow before the John Galt statue downtown with sufficient enthusiasm. Maybe they were conspiring to bomb a Galtonic lodge. It could be just as likely that they were needed to fill a monthly quota for arrested subversives. Who knows? There are so many maybes. These days it doesn't take much to find oneself a victim of the roulette wheel turn of fate unless you're really on the right side of history. If you think about what's happening a lot – which I don't recommend by the way – Sean and Debbie are abstractions dumped into the sacrificial grinder so many can feel vindicated and boast they are on the right track to restoring history. C'est la vie." Penelope noticed his cadence was that of an insurance adjuster reading back an actuary table yet it was strangely compelling.

The undressing

Penelope didn't move, couldn't think, and dared say nothing as he took his rain coat off and handed it to her before sitting down. Without thought, she stood up, took it from him and hung it up on the coat rack in the waiting room. She wondered if it was wise to defend Sean and Debbie Linson or perhaps even ask for a form of clemency from Mr. Jones if he had inside knowledge, the type of power that could help them. What she didn't know is that Mr. Jones had signed their arrest warrants the night before and could at any minute sign off on their executions. Then she thought better of it and said nothing.

"We live in most challenging times, don't you think?" he said. "We are ruled by the Galtian Imperatives but they are unwritten and nobody understands what the rules truly mean."

"What matters is that we believe, is it not?" Penelope replied.

"That is true. I am proof, you are proof and the evidence is all around us. Look at your business, taking in stray souls and giving them a boost of courage or optimism, even hope. You provide valuable services in trying times; yes I think you do, Gretta." Mr. Jones pronounced her name Grey-tah and it echoed inside her brain. She felt he was beginning to undress her and strip her naked of pretention and disguise.

"I am in the security business, which shouldn't surprise you in the least, Ms. Gretta Brecht of Dresden and later East Berlin. It took a lot of work to track down who you are or were." Jones took a compcom out of his pocket and looked at it. "We thought it was interesting that in our personal data compilation report about you we could find so little, so very little. No compcom patterns of usage, no information about buying, not even a good read on your televinet choices. You have one but rarely seem to watch it or use your compcom to do anything but minor business tasks.

Odd, we thought. That is until we discovered you were sky connecting most ingeniously through a proxy name and service. Why would a person do that these days unless they were hiding something?"

Penelope could only take a deep breath.

"It took us more work because you do cover your tracks well, Gretta. Or should I say Lolita and your naughty mortgage scheming ways. Bad, bad girl. Did you know the FBI was on your trail for a long time?" Penelope betrayed nothing or at least she thought she had shown nothing after he had named her first fake persona. "So we went back to the beginning as far as we could. Well what do you know? You were a onetime informer for the Stasi in the 1980s. You see I've learned a thing or two about you, especially after I requested that young reporter interview you. I watched the footage and was impressed with your ability to change the flow of the conversation with little effort and appreciated the titty show you gave him. You were already on my watch list, we already had a file – or Akte as I believe it's called in your native tongue – on you because what better place than a psychic's shop to be a hub for exotic, perhaps even subversive information. But there was little else about Penelope and her alter egos. I was very curious and intrigued, to be honest, and so after our data mining expedition failed to turn up much, I decided to get out of the office. I don't do that often, but you are a rare breed and I wanted to size you up for my own personal file." He paused and asked her for a glass of fresh liberty water.

"You need not fret much for the moment. It's to your favor that I think you're aboveboard, which isn't easy these days. You are a con artist who has found a good livelihood in a legal con. Some may consider you a parasite, but my hat, as they say, is off to you. You found quality paperwork and at least two professional level legends that I know of. You are a survivor and entrepreneur and that is admirable in these unstable times of readjustment. Politics has never been your thing, am I right?" Penelope nodded in the affirmative. "I imagine living in police state dictatorship can squeeze those political ambitions out of a creative person such as you."

Penelope tried to remain calm, tried to envision a con's way out. "It's clear you know much about me so perhaps I could learn how to help you, personally or professionally?"

"No I think not. I'd rather talk about your past and your future, should you make the right choice." He paused and gazed at the crystal ball sitting on the shelf of a tall bookcase filled with Ayn Rand titles and books about John Galt and Ayn Rand and still more books deciphering the great thoughts and deeds of John Galt and Ayn Rand. "I hear you do a smashing channel job of Rand and her creation Taggart. I never got the attraction myself to this new religion and especially turning a cardboard cut-out like Galt into an Olympian hero for the ages." He paused and shrugged his shoulders. "Religious belief is a mysterious thing, especially when illogic disguised as reason has been taken to its extreme."

Penelope looked again at him and nodded in the affirmative. Few openly dared to speak even remotely ill or slightly dismissively of Galt, Taggart and Rand unless they wanted to get arrested by subversive thought militia units. On the other hand, she wished Mr. Jones was more a zealot because at least that was predictable.

"Why don't you channel Galt?" he asked.

She considered. "Galt is God, God-like. I can't channel God and wouldn't channel Galt. That would be, ah, heresy, don't you think?"

"Maybe. I find it remarkable with each passing day that Galt became more real than reality itself, but maybe that is part of our magical age."

He paused. "People want action; they crave decisive measures as the world falls apart. Perhaps you see people on the verge of homicidal rage because the real world isn't conforming to their Galtian fantasies about what the world should be. I believe it was Taggart who said or thought 'it's cracking to pieces, like this, all over the country, you can expect it anywhere, at any moment.' I don't believe in the Randian claptrap myself but like the Bible, it's good for business to know the references and sayings of our good Chairman Galt."

She nodded again in agreement.

"But we digress, don't we, Cathy Delison?" He had just named her current identity but that was no secret. "You were a Stasi informant and that's a good card to play with me. I'm amused by the fact that you not only informed on your parents and your brother but, unbeknownst to you at the time, they also informed on you. We studied Stasi methods and logic for so long that, frankly, I came to admire their work. From a security perspective, there's something admirable about developing a country full of informers ratting out their neighbors and family members. On the other hand, it doesn't do much for creating strong family bonds, don't you think?"

"I've tried to put those days behind me," she said.

"We are talking about your future and what might become of you, so it's important that you pay attention. I think I will like working with you because you have street smarts and are expert at reading and getting people to do what you want. From what I hear, your clients come out feeling less burdened. I'm sure they talk a lot, don't they?"

"Yes." Actually, she thought, the younger militia types and mid-level RAP political officers couldn't shut up. "There are many people in need of help, in need of reassurance."

"You're bullshitting me but that's all right. Just to be clear, I highly recommend you not try your craft on me. That could have dire consequences."

"I just would like to help you."

"You will in good time. First, let me tell you, and I am not boasting here, that I am a product of our new entrepreneurial utopia in which the free market has been unleashed. I got trained by the old government of our crumbling country to do many things, most of them quite dark and nasty. Intelligence, gathering it and manipulating it, is my forte. Privatization has been good to me. It's actually made me quite rich and I have almost no accountability to anyone as long as I do my job well, which is all any good businessman wants. My company provides the best intelligence on subversive activities to my militia clients. I handle intelligence for 63 militia units in the west and southwest and you will help me with five in our happy neighborhood. In case you are curious, the business I run is hidden beneath so many layers of corporate filings that honestly I couldn't find it unless I was really looking for it."

"It sounds as if you have a good business." She felt foolish attempting small talk with Mr. Jones.

"Business is booming and I have become a job-creating genius, a Guardian of Galt. Now that corporations have the freedom to issue their own arrest warrants and provide their own standard of justice to political, media and criminal elements who mean them harm, I am a valuable resource. Why should taxpayers be bothered with local police or silly government agencies like the FBI when we can feel better that the private sector is on the case, charging them more and with no accountability? I mean, really, it would be hard to invent the scenario we inhabit, don't you think?" He paused and took sip of water. "In case you were wondering, I pay in RAC cash so don't bother with paying taxes.

Nobody else does these days and why should they even think about taxes with the IRS now a castrated bunch of pleading windbags. Funny, but isn't that pretty much what everybody thinks of the barely alive government carcass in Washington?" Penelope nodded in agreement.

Making the right choice

"I'll let you in on a significant tip. We are seeing a shift in marketplace demand," he said. "It's happened so fast but it seems we have either eliminated or sent into exile up north the most virulent of the liberal, do-gooders and conservative appeasers. There's a bonus for those folks but I need good gossip, rumors and hearsay on the financial maneuvers of militia fellow travelers and RAP members. It seems we are entering the purity phase of our glorious experiment in liberty without boundaries and there's nothing like a good internal witch hunt to keep the fervor high. Kind of like the French in 1793 or the Bolsheviks in 1918 searching for anti-revolutionary enemies high and low. I suspect a lot of heads will roll so it's best to be on the right side of this nasty equation."

Penelope had no choice if she wanted to keep her head from the chopping block. Mr. Jones controlled all the cards, the table and most potential outcomes at this moment. She knew it and he knew it. She hoped against hope that he did not know that she was a spy for the Germans and the British. He must know, she thought. How could he not know? She wondered and hoped that she wouldn't be executed and thrown out of an airplane to the sharks.

"One of my jobs is to keep track of and keep in line the clowns, carnival barkers and cutthroats among us. For those who do their jobs and stay out of trouble, there is much opportunity if you have the right protection," said Mr. Jones before handing her a handwritten list of suspects she was to inform on. Penelope realized she was now being protected by

Mr. Jones, which didn't make her feel any safer. She looked at the list of names. One was a former postal clerk suspected of being a double agent, three others were mid-level militia executives and the fifth name stood out. It was Jason Bravtart. She handed the list back to him.

"Bravtart is a specialty project courtesy of an out-of-state client. We know you have a good relationship with Bravtart's wife, Sandy. She is a well-regarded militia official and comes in two, three days a week, I believe." She nodded. Of course he knew how often Sandy Bravtart came in. He seemed to know everything, which meant he had surveillance on her and was tapped into her office televinet line. "It's her husband, that ambitious televinet producer that has some people nervous in Texas." He paused. "Do you know anything about what Bravtart is up to?"

This was a crucial decision to make and Penelope did so with little hesitation. She figured Mr. Jones knew what she knew and likely had calculated what she was going to say and that he knew that she knew it. She threw him an easy bone.

"Sandy told me last month about an investment and entertainment plan called the Execution Channel. I think that is the name. She explained a little about how Jason is working on a big deal for televised executions of criminal and political elements with the Texas governor and some mysterious financier she said she couldn't name," Penelope said. "She was so excited and figured Jason would become a hero because it would change the course of history and make them very rich in money and glory. Sandy thinks the world of him."

Mr. Jones looked approvingly at Penelope. "Very good. That's not public knowledge yet but it will be very soon. I would have been very disappointed had you not grasped the tentative nature of our relationship but you passed this test." He left unsaid but surely understood that he would have her arrested had she not chosen to dance this tango. He put his business card on the table. "We will talk more soon. For now, send me daily reports via this secure televinet line to my care. I want detail, always detail." Mr. Jones took a final sip of water and stood up. She helped put on his overcoat and he mumbled something before departing. Penelope noticed the indoor chimes began to chime again as soon as he left.

Penelope quietly took a deep breath. This is manageable, she thought. This can be done. I need to find an escape hatch, she thought. She also needed to find who Mr. Jones was because he held her life in his hands. She wanted to develop her own Akte on him and discover his story. It was also time to start looking for a new identity and develop exit strategies out of the SoCal Liberty Territory. America the crumbling was becoming America the too dangerous for her.

Yet, Penelope felt a surge of confidence. It took some time but by the end Penelope had locked in on Mr. Jones and felt she had a strong read on him. He had strutted too much like a peacock, she surmised, and there was more bullshit and bluster to him than he wanted to portray. His look and routine perhaps disguised the fact that he was middle management material at best and she suspected he was in over his head.

And then she realized what Jones had mumbled. It was Vishnu from the Bhagavad Gita that her old friend Professor Levster had encouraged her to read years before. She shook her head. "I am become death, the destroyer of worlds" was what Jones said.

Penelope felt her assessment of Mr. Jones was correct. He was truly full of himself.

CHAPTER NINE

THE CHOSEN ONE

"Think about it. We have life, death, immense private profit and a modest public revenue boost. It doesn't get any more substantial than that."

– JASON BRAVTART

B efore the Execution Channel became one of the most profitable business ventures ever devised, Jason Bravtart had to make not just a smart pick but a perfect one for the first ExSub, or Executed Subject. It had to be someone with a great story that could be manipulated to maximum advantage. Bravtart found his story and his man in William Notman.

When three guards escorted handcuffed Texas death row inmate Notman to the only interview room at the recently renamed Tritorn Foods Death Row Recreation and Revival Center at Final Justice Stadium, Notman didn't know he would become a star. Given that he was an innocent man on his way to execution, it was understandable why Notman would be skeptical about any possible good fortune coming his way.

After Notman sat alone for 15 minutes, he wondered what was happening. No family visits were scheduled for the day and his lawyer wasn't supposed to stop by for another week. Not that there was much to say or much time to say it because all his legal appeals had been exhausted.

Notman of course, did not know that Gov. Lawrence C. Bowie had a conflict of interest in hastening his execution. Notman also did not know that the actual murderer, his former high school classmate Drew Sininger, who had accused him of taking part in the murder of a convenience store clerk, wanted to recant his testimony and claim it was a lie forced on by police investigators. Before he could do more talking or recanting, Sininger was put into solitary confinement where he would remain until Bowie could eliminate him as a potential problem.

Jason Bravtart did know these facts of the William Notman case as he stepped briskly into the brightly lit room. Like much of the special wing for condemned prisoners awaiting their chance to become Execution Channel celebrities, it had been hastily constructed and the room was only furnished with two metal chairs and a primer gray table. The smell of newly dried paint was discernible. Bravtart sat down and Notman eyed him warily.

"Who are you and where is my lawyer?" Notman asked as Bravtart removed his sunglasses. The producer sat down, pulled a thin folder out of his briefcase and laid the folder down on the table. He looked Notman square in the eyes and wasted no time getting to the point

"I've heard and read a lot about you, Willie, and I don't think it would be exaggerating on my part if I call you a lucky man." Bravtart paused partially for effect and partially because he was excited this moment, a moment of truth and historical consequence had finally arrived. Notman didn't know that three cameras were capturing the interview for a pre-execution show material. "You are going to be executed in 11 days and I'm here to make you a deal. I want to make your death worthwhile and profitable for your family while serving a higher free market good for Real America," Bravtart said.

Notman wasn't sure what to make of Bravtart's opening salvo. He was puzzled but felt enough anger to tell Bravtart "do not call me Willie." Bravtart was briefly caught off guard and asked what he should call him. "I prefer Will. William is fine, as is Mr. Notman. If you call me Willie again, our conversation is finished. I might be a dead man walking to you but don't call me Willie again." Bravtart nodded but Notman continued. "Did I make myself clear?"

"Yes, Will, you made yourself perfectly clear," Bravtart said and realized that finalizing this deal was going to be slightly more challenging than he envisioned. But he quickly returned to the matter at hand. "This is a unique and, I'm sure some will later say, historic conversation and I want us to start off on the right note."

Notman continued to stare and shifted himself in the chair. Before Bravtart could continue the presentation, Notman asked "You said I'm lucky? What do you mean lucky? You didn't answer me earlier – who are you and where is my lawyer?"

"My name is Jason and you don't need lawyers anymore. What you need is a good producer," Bravtart said. "It's a new world out there and justice is going to be served." Bravtart paused as Notman's stare evolved into a glare. "Let me explain, in case you have missed the headlines of the past year. Our great Liberty Court rid us of all that legal appeal mumbo jumbo. You are going to be executed, William, and there's no stopping that train from leaving the station on time. I'm pretty certain that I will be the last new friend you will ever make and so my advice to you is to listen closely."

Will sat back in his chair and pulled at the handcuffs chained to the table and then slammed his hands down. He called for a guard to get him out and glared again at Bravtart. "Whoever you are, I am not a fucking idiot so at least show a hint of respect. I know there are no appeals and they are going to murder me even though I am innocent and anyone with one ounce of intelligence knows it. What do you mean by producer and maybe I don't want any more friends. I still don't what you are doing here."

Actually, Notman knew who Jason was but savored the chance to toy with Bravtart who thought he held all the psychological cards. It was a common oversight of most outsiders who presumed prisoners were stupid or uninformed. Will did know what was going on and had heard rumors about televised public executions and that he and his fellow death row inmates were being sized up for maximum public execution appeal. Notman took a deep breath and stopped the charade.

"You are that execution televinet producer, aren't you?"

"Yes I am. I'm the founder and co-partner in this wonderful free market exercise that is unfolding. If it wasn't for me, if it wasn't for us, you wouldn't be at this fine renovated palace of justice and that's an important point." Bravtart paused and then continued his pitch. "Will, I promise to send you out on a higher purpose, one that will enrich your family some and make you a man for the history books. I know you may not think it possible, but the day of the hero has not passed."

No habeas corpus here

Thus began the next step of The Execution Channel with Will Notman being the chosen one, the first condemned inmate to take center stage. The public was told that Real America Republic of Texas prison officials and Execution Channel fans had chosen Notman through a combination lottery and a televinet public poll from the Top Ten (of 1,259) death row inmates who were waiting in line to be hanged, electrocuted, shot, gassed, beheaded, impaled, eaten alive by lions, burnt at the stake or torn apart by a specialty breed of man-, woman- and child-killing Rottweilwolfs. It was not true. Notman was chosen by Jason because he was innocent and therefore had the best story line to exploit.

Oh, what a lucky man Notman was, Gov. Bowie thought as he watched Bravtart and Notman from an adjacent room. Bowie was sitting in a producer's chair with his name on it, watching this first interview on three monitors. He was particularly interested in the close-up shot of Notman's angry face, which would soon grace thousands of televinet promotional spots as the man who would go first.

If truth be told, Notman intimidated Bowie. He had turned down a pardon request for Notman without a second thought even though there was irrefutable evidence that Notman had not killed anyone and had not even known that anyone had been killed. Notman didn't confess even after he had been questioned and roughed up for 26 hours straight following his arrest. Notman's calmness in the face of injustice had unnerved Bowie.

On the one hand, Bowie thought it had been bad luck that Notman had unwittingly driven a former high school classmate named Sininger to a North Houston convenience store two years earlier. Sininger was an ex-con with a lengthy rap sheet and had been released on early parole due to state budget cuts. He had been walking down the street when Notman, who worked as the head of a non-profit organization that dealt with job and economic development issues, saw him and offered him a ride. For no particular reason, he asked Notman drop him off at a nearby convenience store and Notman drove away. In a two-minute span, Sininger shot the female clerk in the head and grabbed $38.26 from the register. He had also done everything but pose for the security camera in the store and he was easily recognized when police showed his photo around the neighborhood.

Sininger had been caught within hours and confessed quickly. He pleaded guilty and, in exchange for a life sentence and at the spirited insistence of the local prosecutor who was mounting a run for Congress, he fingered Notman as the "white-hater" mastermind. "He loved those Black Panther dudes from the 1960s and said that offing whiteys would be righteous," Sininger said at the trial. "He was one bad dude, always talking about social justice and standing up to power and helping the poor vote and get their due."

When he took the stand in his defense, Notman testified he said no such thing to Sininger and that the state was pushing the ex-con to lie to ratchet up the stakes in an otherwise cut-and-dry murder case. "Don't look at me," he said to the jury. "Who has the most to gain by this circus of a trial?" and he pointed at prosecutor J. T. Robbins who was running for Congress and been recruited by Bowie.

The said prosecutor couldn't muster up much of a case against Notman beyond the perjured testimony of Sininger. Notman had no criminal history, was a college graduate, a decorated Army officer who had fought in the Afghanistan Wars and a highly regarded community man in Houston. It didn't matter. Robbins convinced the jury that Notman was a "Black Panther wannabe and a criminal mastermind" involved in the cult activity of community organizing who had rejected the Galtian Imperatives and had betrayed Real America. "There is no doubt of this man's guilt. The only questions you should consider are how many crimes did he commit and how many more will he commit? We can't take a chance on finding out," said Robbins, who was indeed elected to Congress later that year and took Bowie's seat on the Imbecile Caucus.

When Notman's defense lawyer objected to the logical farce of the prosecution, the trial judge who was up for reelection overruled him and said the presumptive statements were relevant because "we must bow to the superior priority of the Galtian Imperatives." When the defense lawyer asked the judge to explain "such mind-boggling judicial nonsense," he was cited for contempt of court and dragged from the courtroom. The jury found Notman guilty after two hours and five minutes of deliberation and sentenced him to death. It would have been a shorter deliberation but the jury lingered to get a free lunch. Riots in three Houston neighborhoods broke out upon the news of Notman's conviction.

When the newly formed Liberty Court in 2017 let the states eliminate the appeal process if they wanted, Notman moved quickly to the front of the execution line. This group of recently convicted death row inmates was the first sorted out by a new prison software management program that assisted officials in setting up execution timetables. The statistical analysis by the developers of ExeCute Software determined it was more market efficient to execute the recently convicted first because they would be harder to control during their first few years on death row. Those who had been on death row for a long time were considered more docile and easier to handle. No one had tested this hypothesis, but the kickbacks were good enough for Texas private prison officials appointed by Bowie.

Notman had one last chance to avoid execution, but Bowie wasn't giving him a pardon. "Who am I to question the judgment of a good Real American jury and stop the wheels of justice?" Bowie said in denying Notman's pardon request. "We don't believe in so-called habeas corpus around here. Notman must face the ultimate justice because he has earned it."

The Execution Channel lottery had been less about good or bad luck for Notman than the perfect solution for Bravtart and Bowie. They had picked Notman in part because he was innocent and had a compelling life story. Bravtart was rightly convinced that the circumstances surrounding Notman's execution would stir national controversy. Blanketed news coverage was guaranteed, along with sky-high ratings. From a publicity standpoint, Notman was the perfect match.

After two weeks of researching more than 560 possible deat
victs for the first Final Justice star, Notman easily stood out.   ..ave
ourselves a winner," Bravtart said after talking over the Notman choice
with Bowie. It was a favorite phrase of his, one that went back to his
days as a guerrilla filmmaker standing up to the corrupt core of the
liberal establishment that he wanted to eliminate. His groundbreaking
propaganda had seized the public imagination and taken down a wide
range of targets – politicians, nonprofit social agencies, entertainment
executives. In 2015, Bravtart even bagged a Republican Party senatorial
candidate from Alabama who was defeated by a RAP challenger after he
was caught on camera in an unguarded moment. The Republican sealed
his own career fate when he said John Galt was a fictional fraud and
didn't deserve a statue next to the Washington monument.

Bravtart's career, which once seemed on the irreversible decline, had
now reached incredible heights. He was a producer on the biggest stage
of all. "Think about it," Bravtart told a reporter from Entertainment Real
America. "We have life, death, private profit and a public revenue boost.
It doesn't get any more substantial than that." Sandy had helped fashion
the quote and it became part of his standard presentation to advertisers
and corporate sponsors.

Later, when Bravtart was questioned by agents he thought were from
the Bureau of Real American Investigation, he excitedly told his interrogators that Notman was a very inspired choice. (It should be noted
that Jason was forthcoming because he thought he it was a case about
the quantity of Execution Channel kickbacks.)

"It was perfect actually – all the ingredients for a monumental cultural
moment and a ratings hit. Due to software processing, Notman was part
of a group in line for a quick execution. We called it last tried, first
fried," Bravtart told investigators. "This was final and fast justice at its

best. The race angle was obvious. A black man convicted of killing a white woman in Texas still gives Real American people the jitters. The innocence angle was a nice touch showing that for justice to be profitable, it can't discriminate between the guilty and the innocent."

Bravtart also took another track when dealing with the media in the days leading up to Notman's execution. He told RAP repbloggers digging into Notman's past that Notman was as dangerous as could be imagined.

"He is a moocher to the core. Here we had a college-educated decorated veteran of the Afghanistan wars who chose an unrighteous path. He registered voters and worked with corrupt unions to harass our Guardians of Galt. He became an angry community activist who claimed Ayn Rand was a con woman, John Galt was a fraud and that workers should organize for better wages," Bravtart explained. "This guy had a long ugly rap sheet. In his office he had a poster disparaging Real American values that said 'Limitless Liberty = Infinite Stupidity.' We really couldn't have asked for a better stereotype to stoke public outrage for a greater Real American good."

CHAPTER TEN
TRAPPING MR. JONES

"Spies cannot be usefully employed without a certain intuitive sagacity. They cannot be properly managed without benevolence and straightforwardness. Without subtle ingenuity of mind, one cannot make certain of the truth of their reports."

– SUN TZU, THE ART OF WAR

P enelope went right to work after her first meeting with Mr. Jones. She bet that Mr. Jones would underestimate her resourcefulness despite knowing her resume. Mr. Jones assumed he had all the leverage – namely arrest and likely death – over Penelope but she was no fool and quickly decided that his overconfidence would be the weakness to exploit. Mr. Jones suffered from power madness, she thought, and she had options. She knew how and where to find kindred spirits in a subterranean culture of computer hackers, safe house providers, document forgers, transporters, black marketers, rumor spreaders and gun runners. This growing resistance group was anti-ideological in nature and mostly anarchistic towards the reigning or rising powers that be. Penelope's new friends operated in plain sight, often as double agent entrepreneurs working for and often subverting the same operations of militia groups.

Within two weeks she had given material to Jones that seemingly satisfied his information need. She said one militia leader was desperately seeking a séance with his beloved grandmother, another was very concerned about his promotion prospects and yet another leader promised Penelope full protection if she became his full-time mistress while he also complained about the growing lack of money-making motivational purity among his subordinates. She couldn't give any information on another name on Jones' list because the postal clerk suspected of being a double agent for the federal government in Washington had missed his appointment. Penelope suspected he had either bolted for a politically friendlier climate or had been arrested.

The pending launch of the Execution Channel had become the most-talked about topic in the country and Jason Bravtart was a hot commodity. At least for a while, Penelope wanted to maximize her usefulness to Jones by giving him a mix of mostly benign and potentially damaging information about Jason Bravtart. The benign material Sandy had shared about finances and Jason's transformed spirits was truthful.

The corrosive material Penelope conveyed to Jones was intentionally obscure, speculative, difficult to verify but tempting. Was Bravtart frustrated with his business partners? "Sandy doesn't have a definitive answer but I sensed that was the case," she said. Was it true he was solidifying ties with some militia groups in Texas? "It could be true but Sandy wasn't entirely sure because so much was happening at such a fast pace," Penelope reported.

Jones suspected that Penelope was playing a cat and mouse strategy with him but he couldn't be sure. Taking no chances, he decided to remind Penelope of her predicament and sent in one of his bodyguard enforcers named Carton, an unpleasant fellow who slapped her hard twice, knocking her down both times. "Mr. Jones may think you're something special but I don't and I will catch you in the act," Carton told her. She was being watched and was warned not to even think about fleeing for Mexico or anyplace else. "I understand," she said as she applied an ice pack to her bloody lip.

She continued to work on two fronts despite the obvious surveillance. It helped that she had access to a secret and secure televinet system, supplied by a hacker named Z who oversaw digital security for a SoCal militia digital hacking detachment. But Z also worked for an underground resistance platoon that watched and hacked the hackers. She hired a different hacker specialist with the code name of X to reverse engineer most of her security system and, in effect, to show the surveillance people watching Penelope in her shop something that didn't always exist. This protected her most sensitive communications and allowed her the illusion of compliance.

She also calculated that Jones would be watching and he would expect her to set up a secure second televinet link. So she gave Jones one he could tap with moderate difficulty. On this front, Penelope focused on searching for fake investors for a Penelope's Place franchise plan. She communicated with a trio of British agents in Utah and Texas who supplied proper information to make the scheme appear legitimate.

Within five weeks after first meeting Jones, she had secure communications, two new identities and solid legends, expert documentation and British passports. She also was in the final stages of creating exit routes through Northern California and Mexico. Her goal was to escape from the SoCal Liberty Territory within a few months after the launch of the Execution Channel. She hoped and was fairly certain that Jones was none the wiser.

Penelope's spirit's rose when her British and German intelligence sources came through and penetrated the shroud of mystery surrounding Mr. Jones. Penelope called in every favor she could and within a month she was given composite reports telling her that Jones had been a highly regarded black ops manager with the CIA who had branched out into the private intelligence sector. Mr. Jones, who was actually named Doug Bason, had attracted a wide range of corporate and militia clients in and outside of Real America. But, as Penelope suspected, he had been more of an operative than a real manager. He had risen rose to the top leadership ranks quickly and perhaps wasn't accustomed to the view.

Bason's company, the blandly named Supreme Maintenance Services, was indeed buried under layers of shell corporations. Penelope's request to find out about Mr. Jones set off alarms bells in London, Ottawa, Paris and Berlin and changed the game entirely because Penelope would not be alone. She found out that four international intelligence agencies had listed Bason as a Red Flag commodity who was to be abducted or killed on sight and for good reason.

Mr. Jones was connected to the recent murder of two British agents. The agents had infiltrated a massive money laundering scheme involving three British, six German, two French and two American banks; Mexican drug lords and local and national police officials; seven international terrorists; two American governors (one was thought to be Gov. Bowie of the Real American Republic of Texas), scores of militia leaders (including Col. Rufus T. Fairbush), 37 members of Congress, and a well-disguised American company believed to be making hundreds of billions in six international currencies.

It was the largest such public-private criminal scheme anyone had ever seen and a crumbling American government had given up trying to bring it down. The two murdered female MI-6 agents had been tortured and then beheaded after coming close to identifying the American brains behind the operation. Their heads were returned to MI 6 headquarters in London via overnight shipping along with a greeting card that read "don't mess with Galt." The name meant nothing to Penelope, but British intelligence analysts believed that Frimmer Empire Enterprises was the well-disguised American company behind the entire operation but they couldn't prove it.

"We would like to have a chat with your Mr. Jones," said Clive, a senior MI-6 supervisor who had flown in from London just to meet Penelope when they realized who Mr. Jones was. "We think he may have been behind that very unpleasant business you were briefed about. We believe he is supplying intelligence and cover for this operation though to call it an operation is an injustice to its scale. It goes much deeper than that and it's best for you not to know more. We don't want to give the game away. We'd like, no, Penelope, we really require your assistance to secure the cooperation of Mr. Jones. From what we understand of your unique CV, you have the right skills for this important task."

Penelope and MI-6 developed a careful plan most likely to succeed and it was one that demanded patience. It would prove to be the most important role and con of her life. In addition to trapping Mr. Jones, she would also get paid quite well for her efforts and get immunity for all past criminal sins. Most importantly, Penelope felt she had a very good read of the table and the game. "I know who you are Mr. Jones," she said to herself one late night as she visualized the cinematic details of his demise and her escape. "I know who you are but you barely know who I am or what I can do." Now she had to get Mr. Jones into bed.

CHAPTER ELEVEN
EXECUTION CHANNEL, INC.

"Frankly, I'd like to see the government get out of war altogether and leave the whole field to private industry. If we pay the government everything we owe it, we'll only be encouraging government control and discourage other individuals from bombing their own men and planes. We'll be taking away their incentive."

– Lt. Milo Minderbinder, Catch-22

For the creators of the Execution Channel, it all came together incredibly fast. In less than eight months, from the summer of 2017 to the spring of 2018, the combined vision, marketing influence, public financing, private and public corruption, bribery excellence and violent extortion talents of Bravtart, Frimmer and Bowie had put the Execution Channel on the air – first online, via the Real American Wide Web and then on the remaining 526 mediatainment outlets throughout the country who bought shares in the network to get a piece of the action. The 925 million RAC publicly financed execution stadium was renovated in record time as all regulatory hurdles were eliminated to "ensure that Galtian goals of efficiency and maximum exploitation of environmental and labor standards would be met," said one press statement.

The naming rights for the stadium had yet to be sold, but it was rumored that the cost would go as high as 30 billion RAC. Hundreds of millions of RAC were also at stake for corporate naming plans to everything from bathroom urinals to supply closet doors. It was hailed by RAP business pundits as a shining example of public-private partnerships in the new Galtian age, with the public paying the investment costs and the private sector reaping huge profits. Even religious leaders saw the value. "The Execution Channel is providential evidence that our faith in the Galtian Imperatives reaps real rewards," said the Rev. Billy Babson in a sermon to his parishioners in Dallas just after he was named the head chaplain for Final Justice Stadium with an annual salary estimated at 750,000 RAC along with performance bonuses.

The Final Justice Stadium complex, which included the largest shopping mall in Real America, 28 restaurants, and the largest video game amusement center anywhere, led to the creation of more than 15,525 new, low-paying jobs. Officials from other RAP-led states begged Bravtart to sign them up so they could reap the rewards of public executions but after an initial sign up of three states, Frimmer and Bowie decided to hold off until after the first execution. The buzz for weeks was unrelenting as the countdown to the first execution became a public fascination.

"This is a machine, Chairman Frimmer, like a well that pumps up RAC instead of oil," Bowie said to Frimmer over the phone one night as part of their daily progress call. Bowie needed to hire two new personal accountants just to keep up with the deluge of kickbacks coming in from contractors and potential corporate sponsors who wanted in on the ground floor. His personal wealth had increased tenfold and Bowie rerouted state money from EC proceeds, not to pay off the bonds for the stadium but to enhance his own militia.

His rival Col. Rufus T. Fairbush publicly complained about Bowie's power and money grab but Bowie's rise had blunted Fairbush's momentum for now. If need be, Bowie also was becoming better prepared for the inevitable showdown. He'd been warned that Fairbush wasn't waiting for a gubernatorial primary and had decided to take him out, either by an ambush or a drone strike. An attack was likely in the coming weeks.

"It was meant to be and the best is yet to come," said Frimmer, who was actually in a jolly mood, in part because he was using a proxy provocateur to escalate tensions between Fairbush and Bowie as part of a long-range plan to dispose of Bowie. "It's a perfect monopoly." Frimmer was said to be surprised by nothing, but even he was taken aback by the free market-altering avalanche they had unleashed by the impending the Execution Channel. His budget alchemists told him nvestment of almost 1.5 billion RAC would be returned within a few weeks after opening night. Best of all, he was laying the groundwork for the addition of more than 15,627 people to his IP, or Influence Payroll, ledger that would extend far beyond his typical RAP/ New Southern Alliance stronghold.

The prospect of televinet executions had seized the country's imagination. The televinet was abuzz with debate and speculation and investor confidence soared as the stock market topped a record 35,125 Galt Jones mark. Historians said the country had not shared a communal experience like this in more than seven decades since the early days of World War II. It was clear to many broad-minded commentators that the Execution Channel represented a critical break with past, liberal-tainted restraints on true economic development and human quantification.

"It's important, finally, for the Real American marketplace to put a price and ratings measurement on death," said the renowned Randian-market psychologist G. Wilder Soutron. "Our seers of Galtian prosperity now have faith in the proper calculations of measuring life and death value. This will lead to breakthroughs on many fronts as the free market spirit will harvest former forbidden territories of commerce."

Bowie had done his part by seizing through eminent domain and then renovating a former college football stadium. He personally oversaw the creation of the 62,000-seat stadium with great sight lines, some 57 giant video screens and 110 luxury boxes that offered all the comforts of the best sports stadiums in Real America. He pushed the legislature to pass an emergency bill to pay for the renovations at Final Justice Stadium and sold it well.

"This is a necessary economic development project that proves again the wisdom the Galtian Imperatives," Bowie said. He also announced an upward revision of income and sales tax rates on low-income earners to finance the bonding of the project. The bill was also paid in part by a fee for public execution tickets, the leasing of luxury boxes to corporate sponsors and a special prohibitive tax on new and used books, music and movies that did not meet the Real American Values Network seal of approval.

Bowie cited a popular book from the 1960s as an example of lingering subversion that must be taxed. "We believe in freedom of speech but it can't come without a cost. If we must allow heretical books that condone skepticism and disbelief like this cynical book *Catch-22* they should be taxed to finance a greater good. We must condemn the continuing slander and degradation of Army Lt. Milo Minderbinder, one of my personal idols. Minderbinder was ahead of his time, a true Real American hero who blazed a path of free market ingenuity during World War II by cornering the market on Egyptian cotton while forging important commercial alliances with the Germans to secure Polish sausage to trade for eggs on Malta. Milo showed the Galtian Imperatives at their best by cutting a deal to bomb his own people to maximize profits for all shareholders regardless of which side of the war they were on. Such genius should be canonized and those who dare criticize his genius should pay extra for the right," Bowie said in a press statement announcing the opening date of Final Justice Stadium. The date of April 15 was also significant as it was the first Galt Day to be celebrated in Real America and it would replace the former tax day that all Real Americans reviled.

The final sell

Before the country could focus on Will Notman and his starring role in establishing the Execution Channel as the ultimate reality media destination, Bravtart had to get Notman on board and this had become a challenging task. Though he seethed, Notman kept it under wraps and decided to play along to find out what was happening.

"So what's this deal you have?" Will paused, still trying to get the full measure of Bravtart.

"It's funny how arbitrary everything can seem. You're on that side of the table and I am on this side. Who knows maybe I could have been the one giving a ride to a murderer and you could have been a successful Guardian of Galt," Bravtart explained. "But you know I don't believe in that arbitrary stuff, there but for grace of my race and God go I crap. I believe my will informs and guides my destiny as yours did for you."

Notman shook his head. "Let's set the story straight and get the facts right. I got fucked and it had nothing to do with will, mine or yours. It was an arbitrary destiny imposed on me by a racist criminal justice system that has neither brains nor mercy."

"I grant you that may be true but it is not relevant any longer, Will," Jason said in a respectful tone. "You have lost control of the facts and your innocence is no longer a relevant fact. I tell you with all humility and respect that facts are what we say they are and the most important fact right now is that we control your destiny. Why so glum? You are lucky to be the first chosen for Galt Day to make the ultimate sacrifice. If you make the right choices, I promise you proper glory and your family will be taken care of."

"What exactly does this mean? You sound like a second-rate car salesman or a third-rate politician."

"Let's get one thing clear, Will," Jason stated firmly. "I am not a second- or third-rate anything. I am here because of my ideas and my vision and because I have courage of action. I am here, sitting on this side of the table and free to go at any time because my beliefs are not only correct but they allow me access to genius you can only imagine. So you may talk tough but I hold all the cards to your upcoming execution. Have I made myself clear?"

Bowie watched intently and thought this might be the turning point. Will sat silent for 15 seconds, then 30 seconds and then a minute before he spoke. "Your madness is crystal clear but for all your talk about will and action, you have forgotten something. I decide whether you hold any cards over me."

Jason was annoyed. He had expected a much easier go of it and Bowie, watching in the control room, was not happy either. He made a quick phone call to the manager of his special interrogation unit that was currently working on a pair of Fairbush spies they had captured. If necessary, they needed to break Notman and get his cooperation one way or another.

"I'm offering you money, lots of it, for your mother, not just cash but a stop to the foreclosure of her house and enough money to retire on, and jobs for your unemployed brothers," Jason countered. "You will choose how to die. Will it be with dignity or as a common criminal no one will miss a week after?"

Will laughed as though they were speaking different languages. "You know what's funny. They only allow two books in this wing, *The Bible* and *Atlas Shrugged*. It's pretty amazing when you think about it. So I reread your Randian gospel again and actually enjoyed it as suitable entertainment for teenagers who think they have it all figured out, that their shit doesn't smell and their omnipotence is all that matters in the universe. To be sure, Rand doesn't make it easy with her fantasy conspiracies of people state moochers and looters stealing from the enlightened few men and women of industrial action and moneymaking talent. There are too many exceedingly long passages of repetitive idealistic melodrama for my taste. I mean really, who but a lunatic would write a 60-something page speech? Even Plato had more humility. But hey, I admit it's got something for every state of psychosis, even including mine in my current situation."

He paused and could tell that he hit a nerve with Jason who was feeling the need for physical reaction but was too much of a physical coward to actually act.

"Let's close this interview with an appreciation for her juvenile genius. I think I can recite this just right, so here's my answer straight from your goddess herself: 'I will not help you to pretend that I have a chance. I will not help you to preserve an appearance of righteousness where rights are not recognized. I will not help you to preserve an appearance of rationality by entering a debate in which a gun is the final argument. I will not help you to pretend that you are administering justice.' "

Jason was at first startled and then he started putting papers back into the file folder and stared at Notman who had committed heresy by quoting Hank Rearden. This was treason of the highest order, unforgivable ideological blasphemy. "You dare to invoke Hank Rearden? That was incredibly unsmart on your part to compare your pathetic situation with that of a great man of action and success. No one will remember William Notman. You registered moocher and looter voters. So what. You organized scum level workers for higher wages they didn't deserve. Again, so what. You were a community organizer begging for free gifts to the moocher population. No one cares. You are destined for the dustbin of history while Hank Rearden lives on and on as an inspiration and a role model. He created Rearden Metal and risked his life to rescue John Galt. What did you create?"

Notman laughed with gusto. "I want to thank you for this distraction because it takes a certain kind of dementia to deify a fictional stereotype that created nothing."

Hardball

Jason paused to get his balance back. "I tried to reason with you and help lead you down the right path. Say what you will, Mr. Notman, but you should be concerned about making your execution bearable and profitable. I promise that your cooperation is assured." Notman stared at Bravtart. "Your attitude is highly inefficient but that can be changed quickly enough."

Bravtart paused to savor the moment. "We could discover that your mother committed fraud on her home loan document and the dear widow Notman could be evicted tonight and arrested on conspiracy charges." Notman said nothing. "And those brothers of yours, Kevin and Trevor, could be arrested for any number of reasons. Maybe they have displayed insufficient enthusiasm for the Galtian Imperatives or didn't pay their fair share of War on the Poor taxes. Tax evasion by moochers isn't looked on favorably these days. Honestly, who knows what could happen to them if they enter the criminal disposal system. They may be never heard from again. A lot of people are just disappearing these days, just dumped as fish food in the Gulf of Mexico.

"Or none of those scenarios could happen if you see the light and appreciate the advantages of cooperation. But now that I think some more about it, their criminal downfalls would add great material to the biography video we are making for the execution pregame show. That would the crowd screaming even more lustily for your scalp. We could call it a genetic predisposition for anti-Galtian behavior."

"There's no need to make this personal. I thought this was a business negotiation?"

Bravtart looked again at Notman's file. "It's hilarious to see your pitiful effort at organizing and voter registration. Really, couldn't you have used your gifts for better and constructive purposes than stirring up hopes for the moochers? We will win, you know. Even the states that haven't embraced our Real American agenda are lining up to sign Execution Channel deals because they see the innovation and the financial windfall. You will be long dead and forgotten when the Guardians of Galt triumph," he said. "Just as it was foretold in *Atlas Shrugged*, this current state of chaos and destruction is a prelude, a necessary step to build the structure of glory to come. Many will be sacrificed for the common and historical good. We are cleansing our collective soul to realize for the first time this country's promise. If we are ruthless and righteous, if we are true to our genius, we will prevail."

Jason paused again. "Do you know why we will prevail?"

Notman laughed. "I don't have enough time left on earth to properly answer that but right off the top, I would say it's because you are only partially disguised tyrants and economic criminals."

"You laugh and continue to miss the point. We have achieved one level of genius by having people consistently vote against their own interests," Bravtart said. "The next frontier is to have them give up and realize they have no interest whatsoever, all by their own choice."

Bowie picked up his cell phone was told that his political persuasion team was en route and would arrive in 15 minutes. This could go either way, Bowie thought. With each passing day, Bowie had become more impressed with Bravtart who was clearly more than a fancy Hollywood producer type. Bravtart wasn't afraid to apply leverage and he wore his genius comfortably.

"So what's it going to be, William? There is a good deal on the table and if you turn it down, I will find someone else who wants the glory of being the first. You will be put back in line and thrown in the schedule as a preliminary execution that no one cares about and your family will suffer for your stubbornness and lack of vision."

William Notman wanted to kill Bravtart, wanted to strangle him until his eyes bulged out and as he took his last breath, wanted to see Bravtart's bulging eyes beg for help. But that could not happen and he had his family to consider. He figured Bravtart and Bowie would more than likely double cross him anyway but he had to take a chance that he could protect his mother and brothers at least for a while. He realized it was the only justice left to him.

Notman swallowed his remaining pride and nodded his head in the affirmative. He said he wanted the terms of their agreement to be fully spelled out and signed by his lawyer and his mother. Jason smiled. "It's a wise choice, William," he said.

Praising Galt for profit

William Notman didn't know the double cross was already in motion. Notman's lawyer had already been bought off by Frimmer's agents and his mother and brothers would be arrested immediately after the execution. A press release was being prepared saying that the talent contract had been "regretfully invalidated" due to the involvement of the Notman family in unspecified "political activities that run counter to the Galtian Imperatives." Bowie, Bravtart and Frimmer would split Notman's

800,000 RAC death fee – or more depending on which method of execution Notman chose. It was a win-win-win situation and Bravtart was particularly proud of his cunning and genius.

The Galt Day execution date was set and they had their first ExSub. Beginning tomorrow, Bravtart would hit multiple morning talk shows and unveil the televinet videos on Notman that were undergoing their final edits. A week of saturation media coverage would commence and Notman's life and crimes would be analyzed and debated from coast to coast. As he met up with Bowie in the observation room while Notman looked over the contract, Bravtart shook the governor's hand and said "Now let's go make some real money."

Before Bravtart left, Notman asked for a final word about the contract. "Help me understand this. I get to choose my preferred method of execution?" he asked.

"Yes, as you can see, there's a sliding scale. Your family will receive 250,000 RAC for a firing squad execution because, let's be clear, that's a quick and easy way out. But it goes up to 750,000 for being torn apart by specially bred dogs and 1 million RAC for being burnt at the stake. It's important to have choices," Notman said.

"And what's this about last words?"

"We want this to be a thoroughly entertaining and educational Auto-da-fe. We want maximum value for the condemned, those in the stands, and the televinet-watching audience. A panel of judges will grade your final words and your family will be paid accordingly. I think 50,000 RAC is a nice parting gift for saying 'Long Live John Galt' with enthusiasm," Bravtart explained. "You have to choose an inspiring pre-execution phrase that will lift the hearts of Real Americans everywhere and give them a good reason to applaud your courageous exit. I'm sure you know that unapproved declarations will not be looked upon favorably by the judges or the crowd."

"I figured that out," Norman said dismissively. "But 'Long Live John Galt'? I mean, really, he's not now and never has been real. I will look like a purchased phony."

"You just don't get it, William," said Bravtart with the assuredness of a missionary in his ability to convert the natives. "It's all in your mind. John Galt has lived, he lives today in the minds and hearts of our Real American countrymen and he will live forever as a shining beacon of money-making prosperity and progress to our promised land. What matters is that you as a skeptic see the light at the end, pledge your devotion and are well compensated for your change of heart. It's a very transparent transaction and there's nothing phony about it."

Bowie called off his interrogation team and had them return to extracting information from the captured Fairbush soldiers. Bowie wasn't sure if Notman would double-cross them and denounce Galt. After all, Notman had no further stake in the future and Bowie wondered if maybe they could ensure against a double cross. But his business partner Bravtart had all the bases covered. This was his gift. He was counting on Notman to do exactly that because a double cross would make for a greater spectacle and even higher ratings.

CHAPTER TWELVE

THE GLORY OF THE EXECUTION CHANNEL

"I'm not crazy about reality, but it's still the only place to get a decent meal."

– GROUCHO MARX

Just as Jason Bravtart predicted and much to his delight, William Notman ignored the script and incited the crowd just before he was attacked and torn apart by a special breed of killer Rottweilwolfs. When the sellout crowd of 69,286 Real Americans who had packed Final Justice stadium and hundreds of millions watching on the televinet collectively realized the extent of Notman's heresies – his community organizing on behalf of moochers and takers, his traitorous family, and his anti-Galtian record – they screamed for bloody vengeance in the seconds before the hounds were released onto the dirt field where Notman stood defiantly urging the crowd on.

Even though the crowd noise had reached an almost deafening dim, Notman stood calmly and pointed to the crowd. "The Galtian Imperatives do not exist and were created to steal your souls," he said through the public address system. The audience didn't care whether Notman was innocent of the actual crime he was charged with. He was guilty of hating Real America and committing existential blasphemy by daring to question the validity of the Galtian Imperatives. When Notman was hit by rocks, eggs, tomatoes, apples, and other materials thrown by the crowd, he stood his ground and laughed what sounded like the laugh of a madman. As the Rottweilwolfs locked on to their prey, Notman launched one more oral broadside. "You are fools and delusional morons if you believe in John Galt."

Bowie was stunned and felt betrayed that Notman had reneged on a signed contract. He screamed at Bravtart to "stop him." But Jason waved him off and told the director to keep the volume high and the camera pointed at Notman. "This is exactly what we wanted and why I provoked him to double-cross us. Trust me: It's going to explode the ratings. Notman has done us the favor of proving without a doubt before a world-wide audience that he's a traitor who deserves this fate," Jason said with a mischievous grin just before he gave the word to release the hounds. "Now we get to pocket and split his appearance fees and those for his family with no muss or fuss." Bowie still felt annoyed that Notman had double-crossed them before they could double-cross him but he felt better about the extra earnings.

In addition to their special breeding as killers, the three Rottweilwolfs were also pumped up on a special steroid cocktail pharmaceutical to make them even more vicious. Notman stunned the crowd by not running away from the dogs or even standing still but by charging at them as they sprinted toward him. Notman even started biting the dogs before he was mauled to death. "He was like an unarmed gladiator surrounded on all sides," said James Frimmer II who was watching the Final Justice production feed on multiple televinet monitors at his penthouse office with his chief-of-staff Roland Gunner. "It's too bad he wasn't on our side."

Before the hounds overwhelmed him, Notman felt secure he had done the right thing. Notman was not without his own resources and assumed correctly that Bravtart and Bowie would double-cross him but he cared about protecting his family. During the last family visit, Notman spoke in code to his brother Trevor, telling him he wished they could go fishing one more time near their favorite spot at South Padre Island on the Gulf Coast. Trevor paused and said "Brother, that would be cool, wouldn't it?"

When the Execution Channel security observers taping the conversation checked the data file, they found that fishing was something the brothers had done in the past. But Trevor and William had never fished on the Gulf Coast and that was the code for Trevor and the family to escape. The night before Notman's execution, at a large gathering of family and friends at the Notman house, the mother and brothers disappeared, despite the heavy surveillance by Execution Channel security mercenaries. As the gathering continued deep into the night, the Notmans escaped via the new underground railroad set up to provide safe transit to political dissidents and others in danger of the militias and Real American security services. Within a week they had made their way to one of the newly designated Freedom from RAP regions in southern Maine.

Genetic moocherism

Jason wasn't surprised when he heard the Notman family had vanished. "Last time I saw Notman, he was calm, almost too calm," Bravtart told Bowie. Bravtart used their escape as further evidence against the Notman family brand, proof that William Notman's anti-Real American activism was contagious. Bravtart also decided to supersede potential talk of Notman's bravery in death.

He announced on Notman's post-execution highlight show that a new scientific study was being released the next day that showed a common genetic defect in the moocher population. "We have already determined that Willie Notman had that defect and it ran in his family," Bravtart said.

Bowie was impressed by the depth and sincerity of Bravtart's lying. Bowie knew of the study, one that had been cooked up quickly by one of Frimmer's research institutes to stir up controversy and to be used as an Execution Channel marketing tool as further justification for loosening

up capital punishment guidelines in newly franchised states. A .
focus group run by Sandy Bravtart revealed that Execution Channel
supporters wanted to see a greater quantity of moocher ExSubs.

"I really think you should give the Real American public what they
want, more moochers and takers and looters," Sandy said to Jason, who
rarely ignored his wife's advice. That led to a brainstorming session
with Gunner, Frimmer's chief of staff, who then ordered a study created
by the same Frimmer scientists who had churned out research proving
definitively that global climate change was good for the long-term environmental needs of the planet. Based on biblical prophecies and repackaged research from the 1920s, the scientists at the Climate Change Hoax
Institute claimed that reality-based scientists were misreading "signs
from God" and ignoring the peril that a decline in fossil fuel production
would have on the environment.

"We believe that a decrease in so-called greenhouse gases will cause an
imbalance in climate destruction which could accelerate said destruction," researchers testified in support of a new RAP-supported measure
by New Southern Alliance states to increase tax credits to coal and oil
companies that contribute the most to climate change. The study was
celebrated "as a brilliant breakthrough in denial," according to one RAP
science commentator. "We should thank these courageous scientists for
practicing a true science free of political bias. The study respects people
who prefer by habit to maintain their head position in the ground and
hope that the destruction wrought by natural forces we cannot control
will not happen overnight before they can have their apocalypse survival shelters completed. It is better to embrace science that respects
ignorance and superstition than to pretend like the elite that we know
what we are talking about."

Jason was happy to put this excellent cadre of paid scientists on the job to discover and prove the existence of a moocher genetic mutation, which they did after 10 days of pretend research. "This shows the intangible power of the Glatian Imperatives and proves the correctness of our method," Jason said at press conference attended by RAP-approved reporters, bloggers, columnists and representatives of states considering signing up for Execution Channel franchise rights. "Through one great strand of genius we have created multiple innovations in science, research, economics, marketing, and, of course justice, in accordance to the Galtian Imperatives and the Real American way of life. This is change that matters."

An audience hit

Opening night of Final Justice Live was a megahit that surpassed even Jason's highest expectations. He knew he was back on track and had correctly measured the pulse of the Real America.

"The example set by the Execution Channel is exactly what Real America needs in this time of great uncertainty and confused thinking," said an editorial in the Frimmer-owned Real American Times. "We applaud the financial exploitation of the public trust and the innovation that drives it. We question the wisdom of any state that doesn't follow in the trailblazing example set by Gov. Bowie and the Real American Republic of Texas."

Commentators, reporters, bloggers, and the public reacted strongly and ran out of superlatives to describe the opening night of live executions on the Execution Channel. The estimated ratings for night one was beyond anything measured in the history of the televinet and its television predecessor.

"It seems it's all anyone can talk about, think about and watch," Bravtart said on the RAP instachat site during the first Execution Night in Real America telecast. "You want more and more you will get. We promise both quality and quantity and the best in creative executions."

Just as Jason figured, the controversy over William Notman's guilt or innocence was a major factor in boosting interest in his execution and it became an international controversy. Media outlets in non-RAP states criticized the practice of using public money to subsidize private enterprise profits as a "disgraceful scheme meant to degrade and debase" the morale of a country already burdened by deep social, economic and political stresses.

In Europe, there was outright condemnation and one newspaper in Sweden suggested the country offer Notman posthumous citizenship. Furthermore The *Tagesblatter* of Stockholm captured much of the global sentiment and condemned "this peculiar American institution of barbarity and economic exploitation in the execution of an obviously innocent man" and accused Real Americans of putting profits before justice. "Are there no restraints, no reflection on how great the depravity?" the editorial asked.

But Real American Party media outlets went on the offensive and countered all national and international criticisms with defiance. "This is a moral and financial crusade worthy of our support to the death," said RAP columnist H. Jack Lamontoff who posted content on a Frimmer-owned political watchdog web site. "We cannot let political attacks by effete socialist countries from a decadent continent tell us about proper conduct or dare to challenge our Real American way of life or the Galtian Imperatives. The Execution Channel is the right genius at the right time to provide a needed economic boost of innovation and private sector direction. It will bring the country together for a common Real

American purpose of prosperity for those who have the right kind of vision and justice for those who can afford it. We have found the right price point for justice and how best to exploit it for financial gain. This is a profound example of how the Real American economy benefits the few and inspires all with daring deeds of market manipulation. It is clear that what is good for the Execution Channel is good for Real America."

There was one more Execution Channel innovation that was not publicly trumpeted. Despite Bravtart's assertion that they were good for ratings, Bowie and Frimmer decided they didn't want any more ExSub double-crosses. Notman's anti-Galtian rant was fine, but they preferred more docile ExSub final speeches that showed a dying appreciation for the glory of Real America and the greatness of the Execution Channel brand. When Frimmer's research team came up with old vid footage of the Soviet show trials in the 1930s, Bowie agreed this was the way to go. "Those Russian generals and other people Stalin slaughtered seemed grateful to die for a cause, to die for their Motherland and confess their sins in the process. They looked pretty beaten and probably were tortured and drugged, which is what we want," Bowie told Bravtart and Frimmer. "We need a happy drug to send them out smiling and grateful and make them confess to almost anything."

Frimmer had Roland Gunner get the pharmaceutical development team on the case and within a week they came up with just the right serum.

Franchise sales up

Even before William Notman's execution became the most important story of the 21st century, envious states were eager to secure Execution Channel franchise rights. And they were willing to pay hefty prices for the honor. It was a good deal for Oklahoma, Montana and Alabama, the first three states to sign on before opening night. They paid 125 million RAC in franchise rights to get back 33 percent of all revenues. Because they had no money to pay for the franchise rights, the states signed bond deals backed by the Execution Channel and sold by private equity experts who worked for Frimmer. That debt was then resold as a security and then repackaged and sold again as a CMDO, or certified meaningless debt obligation. "The taxpayers of these states will end up paying tens of millions RAC in excess fees but in return they will take part in one of the greatest and safest investment plans in Real American history," said the voice in a televinet commercial urging RAP voters to encourage lawmakers in their states to jump on board the Execution Channel express.

The discount window wasn't open long as investors begged for more. FEE was offered an astounding 38 billion RAC by a core of foreign private equity sharks who wanted to buy the Execution Channel but Frimmer wasn't selling, or at least not until his statistical models showed he was near the top of the bubble. After the first night of Final Justice Live, the state franchise rights jumped to 170 million RAC for the right to have 15 percent of revenues. The bonding costs also rose for the next round of interested states and those taxpayers were told they should be honored to have the duty to pay for this privatization model that would likely bankrupt their cash-starved states within a decade.

Some fearful economist types warned about an Execution Channel "economic bubble" that looked to them like a "massive Ponzi scheme of further and almost complete upward income distribution." But RAP economists and financial wizards, who belonged to organizations and universities owned by Frimmer, dismissed such claims. One ridiculed the idea of a Ponzi scheme and said the pessimists represented the "last gasp of a cowardly remnant tied to a dark past of government dependency, deficit spending and hollow promises of economic growth."

Within three months of the Execution Channel launch, six states had begun public execution programs and there were now four "Execution Night in Real America" blocks each week and the ratings remained at record levels. Frimmer was pleased that his initial investment of 1.45 billion RAC had been paid back and his minions had just completed a special discount purchase of two legislatures in the states of Kansas and Missouri. He had also received an offer of 45 billion RAC to sell his Execution Channel rights.

Flush with cash, Bowie had doubled his militia regiments and was employing a more aggressive plan against Fairbush. One Bowie unit had confronted a platoon of Fairbush protection fee collectors and routed them from the extortion field of battle. Not surprisingly, Fairbush called for all-out war against "Emperor Bowie" and was in negotiations for "an armed assistance front" from members of the multistate Real American Patriot Alliance.

Jason basked in the glow of success and the reaffirmation of his genius, Sandy Bravtart told Penelope the Psychic in one of their last sessions before the founding partnership of The Execution Channel began to fall apart, "He's on top of the world and who can blame him. He has proved the doubters and traitors and looters wrong. Where are the critics who savaged and doubted his vision for *The Real Homeless*? When he is home, there is such joy and profound relief that his unparalleled genius has been shown to be the truth."

Sandy also talked to a militia reporter from Georgia who was doing a feature about prominent Real American militia celebrities. "On those rare days now when we are together, we kneel down and pray together before our Ayn Rand statue at home and realize how our destiny has been shaped by our genius, our will, and our correct way of thinking," the story in the Georgia Minuteman Sun reported. "It's hard to really explain how each day is Christmas Day, full of excitement as we work together on a common goal of remaking Real America. From my side, our new militia protection racket plan in SoCal breaks new revenue records every week as the public yearns for inclusion into the plan. Jason said the accelerated execution schedule proves the Real American public has a huge appetite for infinite spectacle and an appreciation for the morale-building role these exercises in Real American innovation play. The Galtian Imperatives do work and we see it now every day with a continual breakdown of the old ways. What could be grander than seeing one's way of life vindicated?"

Sandy also told Penelope that the Bravtarts had bought a private jet and were purchasing a ranch in Texas so they could commute easier and be closer to the epicenter of Execution Channel operations, which now extended to six states and three countries. But Penelope did not report Sandy's revelations about happiness at home, the new jet and ranch. What Penelope the Psychic said in her report to Mr. Jones set in motion a series of events that altered the course of the Execution Channel and short-circuited the destinies of Jason and Sandy Bravtart, James "Big Stake" Frimmer and Col. Rufus T. Fairbush.

Penelope's play

When Penelope told Mr. Jones that Jason wanted out of the Execution Channel partnership, he was lying in her bed, indulging in a hash pipe hit and not quite believing what he was hearing. "Jason feels he isn't getting due credit and is certain he's not getting the right percentage of the profits. He's also convinced that Bowie and Frimmer have decided to kill the families of ExSubs so they won't have to pay performance bonuses. Jason believes their take will run into the tens of millions of RAC," Penelope told Mr. Jones in a calm, matter-of-fact voice as she rubbed his belly.

Jones was stoned but even he realized the information was dynamite. He needed a careful plan to deal with the ramifications. He immediately called a SecOp manager who checked the digvid copy of the sessions and confirmed the contents. What Jones missed is that Penelope had a tap into Jones' tap. Jones and his people could see Sandy's back but not see her talking. Instead of what Sandy actually said, Penelope and her crew substituted a voice track they had composed that easily passed all available voice detection checks.

"Jason is concerned that Frimmer and Bowie have gotten too greedy and may try to eliminate him from the partnership," Sandy said on the digvid copy. "He's taking steps to protect himself."

"Are you concerned?" Penelope asked.

"No, we have friends in many high places. Maybe it will be Jason who does the eliminating," Jones heard Sandy say when the digvid was re-played. Jones ended the vidcall and sat down in a chair near the bed.

"That is remarkable shit you got from her. I'm not sure if I quite believe it because it makes no sense but with high-stakes business deals like this, you just never know when those brotherly bonds will break," he said. "I need to tell my clients about this first thing tomorrow."

Penelope merely nodded in agreement. It had taken months, but Penelope was setting up Mr. Jones for a fall. Penelope was pleased that either he didn't realize it or believed he was impervious to it. She had never flirt-ed with Mr. Jones in the months since their first conversation. She told Jane, one of the British agent handlers, "I play coy enough, very busi-nesslike and he tries to get informal, asking me about my poker playing days and if I missed it. He asks if I miss Germany or the Germany I grew up with. He asks how my accent is so perfectly Midwestern American and what I would do if a true civil war breaks out. I share little but he asks question after question as though we were on a second date. He finds me interesting and exotic and wants to fuck me or kill me in the worst way, I imagine. I'm sure he doesn't trust me and I do my best to keep him guessing."

Finally, on the opening night of *Final Justice Live* after the execution of William Notman, Mr. Jones showed up at the shop partially drunk. She let him in the door and within minutes they were in her bed and within a minute or so after that, he had done his business. "Like most ambitious Americans who are in over their head, he's in a hurry," she told Sid, a top British agent who had been brought in from London specifically to work with her in setting up Mr. Jones. They noticed Jones' security detail had dropped from six well-armed men to two well-armed men.

Mr. Jones had drunkenly called Notman's execution "the dawn of a new era worth celebrating, a triumph of a strong Real America." Penelope had watched the pre- and post-execution spectacle but turned her eyes away and muted the sound when the Rottweilwolfs attacked and killed Notman. It wasn't an execution, it was a sanctioned slaughter, she thought with disgust. While Mr. Jones was exhilarated by the potential financial opportunities that the Execution Channel represented – most of all, a need for qualified, politically subversive ExSubs that his company could provide for all Real American states – Penelope's emotions ran from to numb to fear.

"I didn't like where this was heading, all this talk of accurate price points on justice and death," she said later in a debriefing with Northern Confederation intelligence officials. "My militia clients had serious mood swings from exhilaration to apprehension. I was concerned about the instability. It was good for business but bad for my long-term survival prospects as more people were arrested following news that the SoCal Liberty Territory had become an Execution Channel franchisee.

One of those was Cassie Blight, a former client and Jason's publicist, who was arrested on charges of 'moocher contamination' when militia intelligence found out her brother was a Northern Confederation sabotage officer."

Mr. Jones continued to visit Penelope's bed over the next few months after the Execution Channel debut and he proved on a regular basis that her premature ejaculation diagnosis was correct. She remained passive for the most part though she joked to him that the growth of his security services empire was matching his sexual appetite. She also noticed that Mr. Jones was becoming ever more careless with his security, which was down to an armed driver and perimeter support from the Venice Beach Patriot Militia detachment. He admitted he was trying to keep affair low-key and make it appear nothing more than the typical running of an intelligence asset.

It was just what the planners of the combined British and German kidnapping operation hoped, especially when they had concrete evidence of his role in the murder and beheading of the two female British agents. They weren't sure if Jones was directly involved or simply passed the agents along to a Frimmer execution team but they wanted him dead or turned into a valuable informant.

Penelope didn't know what would become of Mr. Jones and frankly she didn't care after she learned that her former clients Sean and Debbie Linson had been worked and tortured to death. They had been sold to a militia industrial work camp in Utah as part of their anti-subversive sentence. It was the worst of worst-case scenarios that Mr. Jones had mentioned when they first met. She knew he had lied to her when she asked one day if he could find out anything about the Linsons. "I heard they were transferred to a combined re-education and gun production plant in Arizona so they are doing better than most," he said.

Despite his good intentions, Mr. Jones didn't have a 'first thing tomorrow' chance to talk about Penelope's report. Still feeling a little stoned after his tryst with Penelope, Jones stepped into his vehicle and was immediately knocked out by a stun gun. He and his driver were kidnapped by a combined British and German extraction and interrogation team and driven 15 minutes away to an abandoned warehouse. Earlier, the team had dispatched the hapless militia squad supposedly protecting the neighborhood and made it look like a turf war skirmish with a rival militia seeking to expand into the Venice Beach area.

Penelope looked out window and watched the kidnappers depart, slowly and professionally. It was time to grab her bags and escape north. "Gute nacht, Herr Jones," she said and slipped out the back door to a waiting vehicle.

Goodbye Bowie

Two days after Penelope fled into the night, Mr. Jones gave the report with the false information from Penelope to Frimmer. He was stunned and furious with Bravtart for being an ingrate, for ignoring all that the great Frimmer had done for him and for being disloyal which was a capital offense in Frimmer's eyes. Then Frimmer had an idea, a stroke of genius he thought, and it crystalized quickly. He told Jones to detain Bravtart who was in Texas preparing for the next day's Execution Night in America slate of action. "Get him talking, but don't give him much to worry about. I want to get to the bottom of this before we do anything drastic with him," Frimmer added.

"I'll have my people pretend to be RAP investigators looking into some kind of cross-state corruption ring," said Jones who was relieved to be alive and happy to play the role scripted for him. "We'll get him talking."

"Good. Now get your best surveillance team on Bowie right now. Find out if he's seeing one of his whores and where he is. I think I might have to move up the timetable on another project," said Frimmer, who quickly hung up and turned to Gunner. "Get that fool Fairbush on the vidcon. Now!"

What historians later called the Bowie Ambush had been months in the making when Fairbush and Frimmer found common purpose and decided to rid themselves of Bowie. Fairbush was the key to the first part of the plan when he sent out peace feelers to Bowie and publicly called for negotiations. The goal, a Fairbush spokesman said, was to consider a potential merger of "mutual economic interests" and avoid a divisive RAP primary contest that would likely include a full-scale RART civil war. Frimmer ordered Bowie to make peace with Fairbush because they couldn't afford any distractions that might undermine the many Execution Channel-related financial deals in the pipeline.

Political commentators in Texas and throughout Real America applauded the accommodating tone in the rival camps as a temporary cease fire took hold. After setting a date for merger talks to begin, many commentators believed an agreement would be a ringing affirmation for the New Southern Alliance.

"We encourage Gov. Bowie and Col. Fairbush to keep the Galtian Imperatives at the top of the agenda so as to provide a sure path of solidarity for our new country," said Gov. Benet F. Turbosoin of the Sovereign Corporate State of Louisissippi. This new form of pseudo-government was itself considered a model of new economic innovation when a corporate judge merged the assets of Mississippi and Louisiana after the two states declared bankruptcy.

Fairbush couldn't wait to dispose of a hated rival and Frimmer decided to accelerate his timetable to downsize Bowie. The latest news about Bravtart having second thoughts about his Execution Channel partners was the right opportunity to, as Frimmer told Gunner, "clear the debris and get back on track." They thought they had the perfect trap for an armed drone strike when Jones' black ops unit reported actionable intelligence on when and what road Bowie would travel to meet a mistress (a dalliance that Frimmer had ordered Bowie to halt but Bowie hadn't due to what he called the greater force of "nature calling on me to do my manly duty").

Frimmer didn't particularly care for Fairbush, in fact thought he was quite insane, but Fairbush was willing to do the dirty work and Frimmer didn't mind signing a cooperative contract on this matter. They promised to consider further "business and military ventures" when the legislature appointed Fairbush as His Most Highest Excellency of the Real American Republic of Texas and Associated Territories and Military Commands. Frimmer accepted the agreement as a temporary measure and was already making plans for Fairbush's successor.

Through a special vidmonitor, Fairbush watched Bowie and his top aide Chip Howlen step into the middle vehicle of a convoy. When the moment arrived to launch the missiles that would abruptly end Bowie's term as governor, Fairbush gave the order and said to Bowie "adios, moron."

Frimmer watched via a secure televinet feed as Bowie's three-vehicle convoy came into focus and then vanished in a spectacular explosion. Mentally, he removed Bowie from his thoughts and told Jones to finish his interrogations of Bravtart and put him and his wife in line for the evening's execution schedule. When he turned to tell Gunner to pick a third ExSub to complete the slate, he realized Gunner was not there.

CHAPTER THIRTEEN
A HOSTILE TAKEOVER

"All is for the best in the best of all possible worlds."

– Dr. Pangloss, Candide

J ason was surprised to find himself preparing to meet his Galtian maker. It wasn't supposed to turn out this way at all, he said silently to no one. He felt exhilaration and serenity as he waited to step onto the Final Justice stage. He knew but could not stop the sensations because they were connected to the very potent drugs that were circulating through his body and had taken control of his thoughts, actions and reactions. It has been almost three hours since the doctor injected him and Jason was full of words and feelings but the intense, nonstop conversations taking place were all in his drug-saturated mind. He couldn't speak, he couldn't move from the chair he was sitting in off stage but he was acutely aware of what was going on around him even if didn't make sense.

"Ten minutes to show time, Jason," he heard a producer say. As he waited for his turn on the Final Justice stage, he felt excited, as though it wasn't he who was going to be executed but an alternative version of himself, an actor perhaps, like those he had employed on *The Real Homeless of Malibu Beach*. However, at the same time, he couldn't help but feel satisfaction and joy.

He had reacted with immense pride, not sorrow or shock, as he watched on the televinet feed the hanging of his wife Sandy. He had heard the crowd chant "Praise to God, Praise to Galt" as her body swayed back and forth on the gallows. He thought about one of last technological in-novations he helped devise and saw how well it had worked. As many as five mini-head cameras from multiple angles had shown Sandy's last seconds as she dropped through the trap door of the gallows and fell 15 feet. Jason and the Execution Channel development team were particularly proud that there had been numerous human tests with a newly developed rope fiber to show that was the maximum drop allowed, otherwise the body and head would be separated. The EC sent out a press release hailing this innovation in death as an example of the crossover benefits and technological developments found in the genius of market-based executions and the Galtian Imperatives.

The sellout crowd audibly reacted to her final moments before the trap door opened, her glazed eyes widening, the plunge, the violent jerk, the cracking sound of her neck snapping, and her last milliseconds of life all were captured and replayed in super slow motion. One large monitor showed the medical readings of accelerated blood pressure and heart rate as she dropped through the trap door and then finally a declarative flat line judgment. Jason wondered if the Execution Channel software development team had added these touches to the Final Justice video game that was scheduled for a special televinet release the next day.

A while later he heard the crowd unleash a thunderous roar when James "Big Stake" Frimmer was impaled through his stomach by a lance and then beheaded after undergoing a modified quartering procedure. Again, Jason felt calm and serene, even slightly pleased to get this perspective of the proceedings he had helped create. Jason was impressed that the addition of a one-time-only-use drug cocktail for the condemned, known as the serene serum, was really working. The psycho-hydraulic drug was so powerful that if the condemned was not executed, they would not survive with their mind intact – the brain would literally melt from excessive activity.

The Execution Channel brain trust had learned its lessons from the first executions. Focus group members said they didn't want more William

Notman exhibitions of defiance and defiling Galt. They wanted ExSubs to accept their fate and to repent for daring to defy God, Galt and the Real American Party. The powerful new pharmaceutical did its job to make the most hardened of criminals and anti-Galtian traitors cooperative and mellow as they took their place on their execution stage. The serene serum also quickly became a popular choice for militia and corporate security interrogators unconcerned with the long-term health of the people they were torturing.

Jason sat quietly with no restraints and only one guard standing nearby. Jason was proud that they had dealt with this problem quickly and efficiently. It was a triumph of vision and genius, Jason said to himself. One of Frimmer's own labs had quickly created this cost-effective and efficient solution to the vexing problem of how to get the condemned to act properly before they were whipped, drawn and quartered, stoned, hanged, impaled by a jouster, electrocuted, shot by firing squad or at close range by a .50-caliber machine gun, gassed, beheaded, eaten alive by lions, burnt at the stake, or torn apart by a specialty breed of man-, woman-|and child-killing Rottweilwolfs.

Jason admired Frimmer for knowing how to get things done. Frimmer had been his business partner, the money man who had resurrected Jason's career and historical standing, but now he was dead. That seemed impossible though he had seen it on the monitor that his business partner was now without a head. Granted, Jason thought, they had met in person only once, but he was certain that was Frimmer who had been impaled by a jouster, had a few live organs removed and then was beheaded, his head then placed on a 30-foot pole that rotated around so the cheering crowds could see. He heard the public address announcer say "For God and For Galt. The traitor Frimmer has met final justice for his anti-Galtian crimes." How did that happen? What were his crimes?

Frimmer was supposed to be untouchable, a Guardian of Galt. Jason agreed with himself and said to himself he was supposed to be untouchable as well which made it all very confusing.

He watched Sandy swinging gently from the 40-foot-high hanging stage and smiled thinking she must have been proud to die for the greater Galtian good despite being betrayed. Or had they been betrayed? He couldn't quite remember what her alleged betrayal was and thought it rather odd that Sandy, the most excellent chief marketing officer for the 1st John Galt SoCal Militia, was now dead and hanging. No one had doubted her loyalty to the Galtian Imperatives.

There must have been a mistake but then he thought there were no mistakes, only Galtian progress moving forward in this best of all possible worlds. Sandy and Jason had been on the right side of history and now which side were they on? The question was confusing, and then Jason remembered vaguely confessing anti-Galtian acts to his interrogators and reading from a script how he took part in a conspiracy to kill Bowie and this would be part of the pre-execution video presentation. But Jason didn't consider the confessions real and they mixed in with presentations he had given to advertisers about the market efficiency attributes of public executions.

"I thought it was and then it wasn't," Jason said to one of the nine selves he was conversing with. He struggled to navigate the labyrinth of conflicting thoughts and images and, for a brief time, seemingly a microsecond, he had a quick breakthrough of clarity. "Seven minutes to show time, Jason," the producer said. He willed himself back to clarity and it arrived with the image of Bowie conducting the final interrogation. Bowie?

"How could that be?" Jason asked and then quickly answered, "This was a hostile takeover. Brilliant." It was, he thought, a touch of courageous action on Bowie's part and men of action mattered in Jason's universe. He wanted to congratulate Bowie for his boldness and felt gratitude that he could play a part.

Corporate reorganization

Bowie didn't have time for congratulations from Jason, though he had thanked Jason for the Hollywood Hills mansion that now belonged to Bowie. Jason was a prop in the fourth big act of the day that Bowie had choreographed with not much time to spare. As Jason searched his confused mind for the details of what happened and tried to remember what mode of execution he had chosen, Bowie and his new chief of staff Roland Gunner were in an executive office at the stadium. They were putting the finishing touches on Bowie's nationally televinet speech to Real America that would follow Jason's execution. The speech would highlight Bowie's heroism in uncovering a treasonous plot to undermine Real America.

Bowie would frame the public executions of Frimmer and the Bravtarts for high treason against the Galtian Imperatives as not only good for free market supremacy and efficiency but would hail it as a turning point in the "cleansing out of impure factions" in Real America. He would also announce the necessary seizure of Frimmer Empire Enterprises, which would have a transition board of directors chaired by Roland Gunner.

He would also proclaim a public day of mourning for Col. Rufus T. Fairbush who had died earlier that day "in a cowardly bombing by craven anti-Galtian elements led by the Bravtarts who had infiltrated his heralded militia." Actually, Fairbush was vaporized in a drone strike ordered by Bowie who also had 12 of Fairbush's top lieutenants arrested and executed on the spot. The public was told their complicity with the Bravtarts in "the dastardly plot" to kill Fairbush was beyond question and their executions were vidcorded and posted on the newly rebooted RAPTube subscription service option.

It was an unlikely moment of triumph for Bowie, in part because a few days earlier he hadn't even considered such a radical change of policy or partnerships. He had been happy playing the subordinate role with Frimmer, was willing to hold his nose and deal with Fairbush, and enjoyed working with Bravtart. But it was he who had outfoxed and double-crossed Fairbush and Frimmer before they had out-foxed and double-crossed him. It was an effective hostile takeover, and as with all such ventures, there were casualties.

Frimmer and Fairbush were completely fooled. They couldn't imagine for even one moment that Bowie himself had supplied the intelligence that Roland Gunner verified and Mr. Jones, who worked for Frimmer and Fairbush, had certified as genuine. They believed their own assessments about Bowie being first and foremost a moron and didn't consider Bowie a threat. For a few moments before Frimmer was arrested and Fairbush obliterated, the conspirators believed their drone strike on Bowie had been a spectacular success. Bowie was sad that the ploy did require the sacrifice of his top aide Chip Howlen, along with Bowie's best body double Steve and seven members of his fourth string security detail.

"It was a necessary sacrifice," he said to Gunner of his deceased supporters. "I hated losing Chip because he was wonderfully incompetent and efficiently corrupt. But his getting in that big ole' car with Steve must have convinced them that I was along for the ride. The silver lining is that with unemployment so high, it will give others a chance to step up and fill the ranks."

Fairbush thought he had watched his moment of triumph come true via a live vidcom feed set up by a forward observation spy. He saw the drone strike destroy Bowie's three-vehicle convoy and he silently applauded his own genius. After getting confirmation, he came out of hiding from his new command and control bunker near Dallas. He was traveling in a convoy to Irving to secure RART legislative support for an emergency declaration that would name him Bowie's successor, along with a new title befitting his historical greatness.

Fairbush was working on the nationally televised speech that he was scheduled to give that night. He vowed to track down the "anti-Galtian parasites led by the cowardly Bravtarts" that had killed Bowie. He also promised to purge the ranks of unbelievers and set a firm schedule to eliminate the idea of government. Fairbush told his wife, Alma, that they would soon be rich beyond their wildest dreams because he was now firmly tied to Frimmer (though he didn't know that Frimmer was already making plans to downsize Fairbush).

"Turnabout is delicious play," the very much alive Bowie said to himself as he looked at a vidmon showing real-time vid from the drone tracking Fairbush's convoy. On another vidmon he watched Frimmer preparing to leave his office, the video courtesy of multiple bugs planted by Gunner and Jones. Bowie smiled and pushed the control buttons that unleashed the four missiles from two armed drones. Fairbush would never know that Bowie's militia division had missile-firing drones that had been hidden for weeks. Fairbush also was carrying a homing beacon expertly placed inside one of his boot heels by a Bowie spy.

"Mama Bowie told me there would be days when you just want to sing and dance all day long," Bowie said to Gunner who had abandoned his post at Frimmer's side just hours before. Mama Bowie had never said such a thing but that didn't matter. "Sometimes you have to pause and appreciate a rare gem of a moment like this when a man dies because his boots were on."

Bowie was set to announce more big news: the militia alliances led by the recently martyred Fairbush were now integrated into the newly-named Real American Militia Network, the largest military force in the New Southern Alliance and on the North American continent. Bowie appointed himself commanding general and named Mr. Jones as his operational security commander.

Frimmer's comeuppance

In less than 48 hours, Bowie had eliminated Bravtart and Frimmer as business partners and taken out Fairbush, his sworn enemy. It was a clean sweep and Bowie credited himself for having practiced great genius with last-minute leadership moves. Frimmer never saw it coming, never thought Bowie had the capacity for such skullduggery. This made his capture easy. Because Frimmer's security team had been bought off with offers of more lucrative assignments (or face immediate death) on Bowie's newly formed Praetorian Guard unit, Frimmer was apprehended leaving the offices of FEE.

At first Frimmer was concerned but did not panic. He didn't know who had kidnapped him and he was trying to calculate how much ransom he would have to pay. It would likely be very high but he didn't mind about the payout though he would deal harshly with security personnel who had betrayed him. He wondered if Gunner had been snatched as well. Frimmer didn't imagine that Fairbush would double-cross him so quickly after their alliance had been established, but it was possible. It was more likely, he thought as he tried to look through the blindfold, that a renegade militia group hard up for money had grabbed him. As noted earlier in this tale, Frimmer was not given to surprise very often but this would be the biggest of a life that would soon come to an even more surprising end. After the car transporting him came to a halt, he was harshly pulled from the vehicle. When his hood was taken off he was shocked to see Bowie, and a smiling Bowie at that, standing across from him.

"But, you're, you're dead," Frimmer said in disbelief. "I saw it myself." He was escorted to and pushed down onto a chair in the middle of a private parking garage beneath Final Justice Stadium, which was soon to be renamed the John Galt Justice Metroplex sponsored by Tri-Mort Chemicals. This garage area was closed off, guarded by a squad of Bowie's crack special operations unit. Frimmer squinted as bright lights were turned on to vidcord the final meeting between Bowie and Frimmer.

"My wife, Linda, told me I looked very alive and full of energy today and I didn't want to disappoint her. Funny how that worked out, ole' Jimmy boy," said Bowie who had never before called Frimmer anything but Chairman Frimmer. "You saw what you wanted to see and you saw what I wanted you to see." He walked toward Frimmer and patted him on the head like a puppy. "How funny is this? Mama Bowie would be very disappointed in you. I thought we had the makings of a longtime business relationship but I find out that all along you were planning to downsize me as though I was a meaningless state worker or one of your former assistants."

Frimmer was slightly taken aback by the reference to his former assistants but tried to gain the upper hand. "I don't know what you are talking about. It was Fairbush, all Fairbush. The man is insane. You should arrest him not me. He only told me about the drone attack after the fact. I had nothing to do with it."

"Fairbush won't be arrested in this lifetime. He has been sent directly to hell courtesy of drone missiles I fired up his ass," Bowie said with a smile. "I hope I have time to tell you about his boot beacon because it's the funniest story. All I can say is good riddance to that lunatic and his gangster organization, which happens to belong to me now."

"Fairbush is dead?" Frimmer said in disbelief. "Then he deserved it, not me. Let me go right now and we will forget this ever happened. I had nothing to do with the attack."

Bowie smiled. "My goodness Frimmer, you really do need to get up to speed and take into account the changing dynamics of the day." Another car pulled into the parking garage. Bowie continued. "You thought wrong about double crossing me. There was no need for it but that don't matter now. You never saw this coming so it serves you right you arrogant prick for underestimating my genius. It will cost you your life and your empire."

"You have no proof I was part of this. Fairbush was a madman, you know that," Frimmer said.

"That'd be true. Fairbush was a madman but I know for a fact he was stupid enough to happily do your dirty work. Let me say that again: your dirty work," Bowie explained. "So help me here, Chairman Frimmer, and maybe we can clear up any misunderstandings, especially of the life or death variety." Bowie paused and Frimmer hoped for the best. "If I did some investigating, you're telling me I wouldn't find out anything about my market efficiency downgrade or the order you gave to have me permanently downsized?"

Frimmer hedged for a second but he wasn't giving up. "That's not true. Nothing of the sort happened. It was just a routine assessment at the time and nothing was final because there was so much upside to your potential. This is craziness. We were business partners making a lot of money and each getting what we needed. Why would I want to join forces with that lunatic Fairbush?"

"Well why don't we answer that question, ole Jimmy boy?" Bowie paused. "Are you telling me I wouldn't find out anything about two secret vidcon meetings with Fairbush?" Frimmer felt his spirits deflate almost completely as one of the vidmons replayed a portion of a Frimmer and Fairbush vidcon that ended with Frimmer saying "do it quick and do it without mercy."

Bowie continued. "I ain't a lawyer but what you say there doesn't match the evidence you presented to me here." Frimmer wished he could will himself to disappear. "I watched both those meetings and by God, I was impressed. You guys were serious about business, making sure every detail in your new partnership contract was buffed up. And, I couldn't believe how much you guys had it out for me and thought I was nothing but a puppet and a moron. Mama Bowie would have thought that so rude."

He didn't want to give in but Frimmer knew he was trapped. Before the soon-to-be former chairman of Frimmer Empire Enterprises could say a thing, Gunner stepped out of the darkness and Frimmer couldn't help but gasp. "It helps to have like-minded friends and allies in the right places because it's become quite dangerous around here," Bowie said.

"You," Frimmer shouted at Gunner. "How could you betray me? I gave you everything."

"I would shelve the shocked outrage about betrayal. Give me a break. It took a lot of arrogance for you to think I wouldn't find out about how my predecessors ended up in Happy Meadows." Gunner said. "You hired my brains and analytic talents and you planned to get rid of me the same way you did to them."

"You're wrong, Gunner. They were weak, not management material and easily replaceable. You were the best of the best. I was grooming you for a top slot, for God sakes man, you were going to run the Execution Channel and be vice chairman of Frimmer Empire Enterprises," Frimmer pleaded.

"Well that declaration is a little late 'cause I got the top slot anyway. For my own good, I couldn't take a chance. I knew what you had in store for Gov. Bowie here and I knew it was only a matter of time before I would vanish as well because I truly know where all the bodies are buried. I think you once told me that 'Nobody is nonthreatening. They just haven't been exposed yet.' I was surprised and more than a little grateful that your interrogation thugs were too chatty for their own good during my security renewal. They thought I was too drugged out to hear them laughing and betting on a timetable when it might be my turn to dig my own grave just like the previous two guys."

Frimmer was silent and realized there was no way out of this except possibly to bribe his way to freedom. He needed to cut a costly deal to save his life and legacy. "I may have underestimated you Gov. Bowie and not fully appreciated you Gunner but…"

Gunner cut him off. "I know what you are thinking but you will not buy your way out of this checkmate Frimmer," Gunner said angrily. "You have nothing to bargain with or bargain for except for maybe a quick death. You taught me well and would have been proud of me, how I assessed the situation and decided that it was your market efficiency which had peaked and your long-term usefulness was cloudy at best. This isn't personal. It's strictly business and good business at that.

Gov. Bowie and I came to a joint operating agreement to hasten your execution and divide up Frimmer Empire Enterprises."

"Today's full slate of top-shelf executions will shatter our opening night ratings rank by a lot my marketing wizards tell me," Bowie chimed in. "We will throw out a few of Fairbush's goons as minor opening acts and then we will have you sandwiched around the Bravtarts for the feature presentations."

"Bravtart? What did he do? You are as mad as Fairbush," Frimmer shouted. It was a lie because he had planned the same fate for the Bravtarts.

"Damn Frimmer, that's a real insult you calling me mad and I think you are being untruthful because I heard from reliable sources that you were getting rid of the Bravtarts as well. That being said, it is a shame about Jason and Sandy. It's not fair but I needed them for a complete conspiracy package, about how the three of you banded together to eliminate Fairbush and then attempted to eliminate me. It was a devious plot to plant serious seeds of doubt about the future of Real America and the Galtian Imperatives. Well, we can't have that, can we? Jason's a good kid and I liked working with him but sometimes collateral damage can serve a great purpose. I lost a favorite advisor today in Chip Howlen, but he was sacrificed for a greater good, namely my survival. I think Jason once put it best and I may be off in the exact wording but he said for justice to be profitable, guilt or innocence can't be factors. After all, in the long run we are all dead anyway, guilty or innocent."

Frimmer had a brief moment of clarity from his predicament and realized he had really underestimated Bowie. He was still in shock about this turn of events. As though caught in a deadly earthquake, he couldn't believe his life's work was coming to an end and that everything had fallen apart and crumbled in the space of a few minutes. The realization was sinking in that he was going to die was suffocating him. Now that he was clear about his own fate, Frimmer had one last concern.

"What about my son?" he asked.

"Ya, I heard about that from Gunner here. Damn, you did keep that a big secret. We are reaching out to his pretty mama to give her the lay of the land. I'm not big on that sins of the father being stitched to the fates of the youngsters' stuff so I promise that no harm will come to your son. He will be more than adequately cared for," Bowie said.

"He will likely come after you when he finds out about the extent of your treachery."

Bowie laughed. "Damn Frimmer, you just don't give up. I didn't seek this current situation but you forced it on me with your treachery, so to hell with you. I was happy to keep executing people and raking in the profits but you got greedier than you needed so that is that. I suspect that boy of yours does have plenty of vengeful genes in him but we will confront that problem when it comes."

Frimmer mumbled something inaudible and Bowie shook his head. "I'm still freaked out some about how all of this went down. I was very disappointed to hear from Gunner here that you thought so little of me and my efforts to make you even richer and more powerful than ever, and look what I got for my troubles. I never saw that coming because I thought this was a great partnership but that serves me right for being so trusting. Mama Bowie said it best: it doesn't take much of an effort to show a little gratitude and appreciation."

Frimmer still couldn't believe that Bowie was alive and that Gunner had betrayed him. It was inconceivable and not part of his master plan. Worst of all, he had to listen to Gunner and Bowie mock him and he couldn't stand the thought of hearing Bowie babble on about 'Mama Bowie' this or that. It had become torture.

"We do want to thank you for your service and appreciate how well you set up your empire, which will be renamed Bowie Empire Enterprises beginning tomorrow. I've seen a summary of the books and I am impressed. You had profits galore across the board and we promise it will remain so with Gunner at the head. We especially appreciate the fact that all those people on your payroll have no idea who has bought them so they will continue to serve me and Gunner."

Frimmer shook his head in disbelief and was wounded by the injustice of it all. He had been so close to reaching a milestone of unparalleled genius and influence and now he felt his life force being extinguished. It had all been for naught. Even worse: his empire was being hijacked by the snake Gunner and that moron Bowie and his name was being removed. He felt a powerful surge of defiance.

"I should have gotten rid both of you earlier," he shouted. "You can't run this because I can't be replaced. You are fools and will destroy what my father and I have built." Bowie smiled and then nodded at one of the guards who slugged Frimmer flush in the face. Frimmer spit blood and howled that his cheek was broken.

Bowie took a hankie and wiped the blood from Frimmer's cheek. "Don't fret about your pain, ole Jimmy boy. We have a good strong drug for that. As you well know, the best thing about it is that we can manipulate the behavior of the condemned, of folks just like you, with all the ease of setting the temperature of an air conditioner. You know you will confess to everything we tell you to confess to and then you will go to your death bravely or as a whining coward depending on what we decide."

Frimmer now felt terror and he started to sweat as he had never sweated before. He realized what was coming and what the drug would do to his brain. While Frimmer's sweat started to mix with the blood on his face, a Bowie military aide entered the area and handed Bowie a compcom. Bowie put on his reading glasses, looked at the screen and smiled. He walked up to Frimmer, bent down and looked at him squarely in the eye.

"Hot damn! We have a script update for you and you will humbly confess that you conspired with the stinking remnants of the federal government and anti-Galtian elements to screw Real Americans. You will also confess that you had planned to fund multiple people's state parties and then make tens of millions in payback when the taxes of Real Americans would be raised and the private property of the makers would be seized. You were leading quite a conspiracy and all behind the scenes which make it all the more sinister and conspiratorial, Chairman Frimmer."

Bowie stepped back and nodded again. Frimmer looked up helplessly as two men held him down and another man in a lab coat walked up and injected him with the serene serum in the neck. It was point of no return for Frimmer and he knew it. The men stepped away and Bowie pulled his chair close to Frimmer who felt the first rush of ecstasy and paralysis. He knew that within 10 minutes he would lose some ability to control his speech and thoughts and would begin reveal anything asked of him; within 30 minutes he would become a parrot, faithfully repeating any script written for him; between 90 and 120 minutes he would lose the ability to talk at all; by the three-hour mark, he would lose all control of his thoughts; and that within four hours if he was not dead, his brain would start to overload and begin cooking. Frimmer knew it all and could do nothing but sweat and await death.

"Don't you worry there partner," Bowie said with a comforting voice. "We got you set up on a factory line schedule of confession and execution.

You'll be dead long before the brain is barbecued. That would be cruel and unusual and we don't do that sort of thing. You should take pride that you will be the first prisoner subjected to a three-course execution, just specially designed for your last appearance on the world stage. First, we have an impaling lined up with a medieval jouster dude on a horse who will run you completely through with a lance but he's a pro at it and will miss your vital organs. We've gotten good feedback from focus groups on this appetizer so this should give the audience a stir. For the second course, we will quarter you some and take out a few of those minor organs, a kidney, liver or spleen for public display. And then in a sign of real mercy, you will lose your head and have it hoisted up on a tall rotating pike. For a final piece of judicial symmetry, and you can thank Gunner for this inspired idea, we will bury what's left of you in Happy Meadows."

Frimmer sat there imagining his demise in detail and could not escape from the images and couldn't believe he would soon reside in Happy Meadows. And Bowie wasn't done humiliating him. Mr. Jones stepped out of the shadows with four other men dressed in black commando clothing.

"Let's get to the next highlight of the dance card. You know Mr. Jones of course. He used to work for you but now he works for me and he's happy about that. Hell, he's just happy to be alive. Unfortunately, I don't have enough time to explain all the ins and outs of that development so I will get to the point. He showed real entrepreneurial initiative under a great deal of stress in betraying you and helping our British friends here from that James Bond agency. I've given them an exclusive 15-minute interview. It seems they'd like to know more about why you insisted on murdering two of their lady agents and then sending their heads back by express freight to London. I guess that was in bad form," Bowie said.

"To make a long story short, we signed an agreement to blame it all on you and reorganize your money-laundering scheme. We added our new spy agency friends to the payoff carousel while promising to keep them in the loop and not kill any of their agents. They were the ones who drew on tradition and asked for the quarter and beheading execution buffet and really, how could I turn down them down. Losing your head seems a touch of poetic justice, I say. You can now thank them personally."

Bowie walked away. Within eight minutes, Frimmer began to tell the British interrogators everything, including plenty of babbling about his son Thom, about his mother Millie and father being so proud of his work and the FEE legacy. "I want to be remembered!" he shouted before spilling many of his secrets. The British agents and Mr. Jones didn't care about family or legacy. "Must be the drug really kicking in," Jones said to the puzzled interrogators who had yet to see the serene serum at work. The intense water immersion therapy later applied to Frimmer was an unnecessary but enjoyable highlight of the session for the British agents.

CHAPTER FOURTEEN

REVOLUTIONS DEVOUR THEIR OWN

"I am assured by a very knowing American of my acquaintance in London; that a young healthy child, well nursed, is, at a year old, a most delicious, nourishing, and wholesome food; whether stewed, roasted, baked or boiled, and I make no doubt, that it will equally serve in a fricassee, or ragout."

– Jonathan Swift, A Modest Proposal

M r. Jones, the new operational security chief of the Real American Militia Network, was glad to have emerged stronger than ever. The decision to betray Frimmer hadn't been an easy one. Frimmer paid very well and gave him total autonomy and Jones also knew that double crossing a client set a bad precedence for future business relationships.

But that could be explained. Frimmer's security services had badly botched the murder of the two British agents and this had threatened his autonomy, his reputation and his life. They had been foolish in assuming the British would back off and, after he was kidnapped, it had taken serious negotiations with the British to convince them that while not entirely blameless in uncovering the agents, he had recommended interrogation and return to England to send a less substantial message.

"I told Frimmer he didn't need to kill them to make a point that MI-6 and the other security services should mind their own business," Jones told his British interrogators. "Frimmer believed he was operating with absolute impunity and disregarded my advice. He went a little crazy. Frimmer was furious that anyone had dared to infiltrate his organization and get close enough to uncover some secrets. He had wanted to make a "Big Stake" statement and wasn't going to be denied. He also 'retired' to Happy Meadows some 12 security personnel who had failed at their jobs by allowing the infiltration."

When Penelope the Psychic assisted an MI-6 extraction team to kidnap Jones, the interrogation was unexpectedly smooth and only a little bit rough. Mr. Jones knew he had no negotiation leverage especially after he was told that his wife, two children and both parents also had been detained. He was told in no uncertain terms that anything but full cooperation on his part would result in the implanting of mini-bombs in their heads, which could be triggered at any time, for any reason. Mr. Jones didn't resist and promised them full cooperation and an opportunity for revenge against Frimmer. Though he was angered at her betrayal, Jones not only promised he wouldn't track down Penelope but was happy to provide exit bribery visas for her escape avenues.

Mr. Jones needed Bowie's protection and cooperation for a double cross to succeed and that was not guaranteed. After all, Bowie could turn on Mr. Jones and win points with Frimmer for doing it. But Mr. Jones had to take the risk because there was no choice.

Bowie was surprised when Mr. Jones contacted him and shocked by what he was told. He had heard of Mr. Jones, heard mostly about his legend that is, and wondered why Mr. Jones would want to speak with him. They talked via a secure vidcom line and Bowie understood quickly when Mr. Jones told him of the plot by Frimmer and Fairbush to kill him and the Bravtarts.

"Frimmer wants to corner the entire market. He said something coy to me, that you had reached a point of diminishing returns for him and that he didn't want to pay Bravtart his 15 million RAC performance bonus," Jones explained. "I'm certain Frimmer will double cross me too and have one of Fairbush's psychopaths take over my business. I heard from a confidential informant that Bravtart believes you are negotiating with representatives from the Northern Confederation and that you are selling out. I believe it was Frimmer and his minions who planted that rumor in my region and maybe you should be worried that this rumor will start to spread."

Bowie didn't know what to think. "Sheit, I heard it but just chalked that up to Fairbush who's always screaming about what a moron and traitor I am. That's why I agreed with Frimmer that it's time to cut a deal with Fairbush and move on." He paused. "Frimmer said this bad blood was not good for business."

"I think something is planned pretty soon. Frimmer ordered me to send a dozen of my best surveillance men to track your every move."

"Well hells bells, I didn't know keeping sight of me was such a growth industry. I wish I could invest in it cuz I'd probably make a killing. All I can say is that it's gonna get awful crowded. Fairbush already has a God damn company of his sociopaths keeping track of every piss, shit, meal and blow job from my lady admirers. I even heard of one psychological report they compiled that says the public is transfixed by my haphazard use of contractions. Damn near pissed my pants. I mean what kind of sheit is that?"

Jones watched as Bowie pondered the implications of this discussion. Jones didn't know Bowie personally but there was no doubt about his legendary status in Real America as a man of bold, free-market action who embraced the cause of enriching himself at every opportunity. He also knew that Bowie had turned rhetorical incoherence into a political strength.

Jones remembered the first time he had heard Bowie's name mentioned prominently. Bowie had caused a national stir for starting a fist-fight on the House floor prior to the 2014 mid-term elections. When a female Democratic member had accused the Republicans and Real American Party members of blaming women for the country's economic woes because they were paid too much, Bowie walked into the House chamber and yelled out that maybe the "heretic from Minnesota should get laid once in a while so she can stop being a hysterical, complaining bitch." Bowie was admonished by the chair and then took a sucker punch swing at a Democratic member who had come in the chamber to defend his colleague's honor.

By the time police waded in, more than 20 congressmen and congresswomen were fighting, and six were treated at the House clinic for excessively bruised egos. Bowie went on television that night and defended his actions. "I invite these cowards back into a ring of action where real men settle their differences. We are sick and tired of liberal libel and won't take it any longer," Bowie said. "They lie and undermine this country's greatness with their weak-kneed programs and pussy whining about social justice and equal pay. Real Americans suck it up and don't beg for government crumbs."

Mr. Jones knew that if Bowie survived he would likely be president of the growing New Southern Alliance with territory from Southern California to Florida, and from Idaho, Utah and the Dakotas to the Carolinas. Out of desperation and calculation, Mr. Jones hoped Bowie had the imagination and ruthless stomach to do what was necessary to survive this situation.

"Fairbush is insane scum and getting rid of his nuisance will be a pleasure. But damn, I thought I had a real partner with Chairman Frimmer. It's so disappointing that he thinks I am on the downside of my worth to him. But as Mama Bowie likes to say, there's just no accounting for the malevolent intentions of others," Bowie said. "I guess we're having this conversation because you want to form a partnership to get us out of our mutual predicament."

"Yes sir," Mr. Jones said.

"We better get to it and get it done right because there won't be any second chances."

Their first move was easy. Mr. Jones had told Frimmer about Penelope's confidential report. Frimmer was outraged by Bravtart's seeming ingratitude and ordered Mr. Jones to detain and interrogate Bravtart. When Jones came back with more information about Bravtart conducting protection negotiations with Idaho militia groups, Frimmer had had enough. "Bravtart is finished. Use that new drug we have if you must, but I want to get to the bottom of this and do it fast," Frimmer screamed.

Less than 12 hours after creating the partnership with Jones, a second defector contacted Bowie. Roland Gunner gave him the full picture, all the details of how much peril Bowie was in. Gunner was added to the partnership deal and everyone had their roles.

"Jaysus Christ," Bowie said to Gunner. "I knew Fairbush was bound and determined to kill me but I never saw it coming from the Chairman. But we can't let that stop us from carrying on, can we?" Within hours, Bowie signed off on a new mutual operating agreement with Jones and Gunner and they quickly came up with an effective plan to deal with all their problems at once. It was then that Bowie told his new partners that he had indeed started negotiating with a reconstituted federal government in New York for an agreement that would make everyone happy. The proposed deal would include an exclusive deal for Execution Channel expansion into Northern Confederation territories while making Bowie a co-president of the country if he wanted it and opening the doors for greater financial incentives.

"Sometimes the devil you complain about isn't all that bad," Bowie said. Gunner and Jones, who were sworn to secrecy about the classified

Northern Confederation negotiations, were given a cut of the potential proceeds.

Bowie had a heavy heart when he ordered Jones to bring Jason and Sandy Bravtart to the stadium for execution. It wasn't easy because he genuinely liked Jason and though he only met Sandy one time, he had wanted to hire her as his chief marketing officer because her work in California was admirable. But business was business and the difficult part about being a genius, Bowie thought, is that tough choices must be made.

"Son, we owe you so much. It's damn unlucky and bad timing you got placed in this situation. I want you to know that we treated Sandy with the utmost of courtesy and respect before she was hung," Bowie said to Jason during the final talk before Jason was escorted out to the firing squad post in the middle of the stadium. He had nothing against Jason and Sandy but in deciding to eliminate Frimmer, he didn't want to share Execution Channel credit and profits with its creator anymore. He wanted to write the official history of the Execution Channel and Bowie didn't want Bravtart around raising a stink about who should get what credit. Bowie would be the last man standing among the original partnership so that settled in his mind who got to write the history.

What matters to the public, Bowie further explained to Bravtart, is that we have high-profile scapegoats and a sure sign of a profitable outcome for Real America. The Bravtarts and Frimmer had conspired against Real America, defiled the Galtian Imperatives and had received prompt and public justice. It was a win-win situation for the survivors.

"You are the best propaganda expert of our time, Jason. I admire it and by God you made a difference in tearing down our enemies and, to your credit, you never let truth or reality get in the way. Surely you can understand why we as Real Americans need this purge and it don't hurt any for a little surprise like this. My focus group people tell me it keeps the public entertained and scared down to their toes. You didn't know what Fairbush and Frimmer had planned for me but it wasn't good. Both of those looters have been administered their just desserts. But speaking for Real America, we owe a debt of gratitude for your sacrifice to make my job easier and make me a whole lot richer," Bowie explained to Jason who looked back with a calm, accepting face. "Now good luck to you and not all is lost. My new psychic in residence at the Statehouse tells me you will soar like an eagle to that great Galtian gulch over the horizon."

Bowie looked into Jason's serene eyes, which registered nothing, and he never knew how much Jason appreciated the sendoff and agreed with all the major talking points. He even liked the idea of soaring like an eagle.

Inevitability of Tragedy

Penelope was watching Execution Night in Real America on the televinet far away in Western Canada. She reacted numbly when she saw Sandy hanging and was surprised a corporate headliner like Frimmer had met his demise. It has been a hazardous and tension-filled three days of travel from Venice Beach in a produce pickup truck before she made it to a safe enclave in Monterey. She was then transported by Canadian agents north across the border.

When she was debriefed by Northern Confederation officials, the Canadians, the Germans and the British, she told a harrowing tale about traveling through "hell." Her timing had not been good because the first major battles of the California civil war had broken out. The checkpoints were too many too count. She and her driver had to pull over to the side of the road regularly to avoid militia convoys and dodge at least four firefights. The produce on the truck became contraband of war and w_ grabbed by soldiers in both militias. She saw numerous weapons supply merchants who set up mobile bazaars at strategic locations. These bazaars were by agreement considered demilitarized zones and opposing soldiers were able to mingle with each other, buy weapons and sit down for coffee and doughnuts before returning to the battlefield. "One of the merchants told us it was good for morale if gun-running commerce was not interrupted," Penelope said.

Mr. Jones did play his part well. At two of the checkpoints she was sure her paperwork wouldn't hold up but each time they were waved on. Jones had supplied them with the right bribery visas and directed them to checkpoints manned by inexperienced militia members that appreciated the extra income.

But other scenes were less benign. "We saw scores, many hundreds of bodies – men, women and children of all ages – lying in ditches near the war zones," she said. "We were told by regular militia that these were the work of special militia summary execution squads that had killing quotas of moochers, takers and looters to fill. We saw large billboards had been stripped of advertisements and replaced with banners urging patriots to do their duty and reading 'For God and For Galt.' We saw the same madness in Galtian zones that Northern Confederation forces had overrun. Slaughter everywhere. It was insane. The main and back roads were filled with refugees trying to get away from the battle zones but terrified of the execution squads on both sides." Penelope was shocked by what she saw. "Even with the help of Mr. Jones, I thought we were going to be shot on the spot a couple of times."

As he awaited his execution, Jason managed to memory access his final encounter with William Notman. It was the day before the big event and Jason had returned for a last visit. Actually, he was spoiling for a

ɔ̃   ᴜse Notman had not embraced the Galtian Imperatives.
             ed a last ideological joust and mocked Jason and the
∪∪......... ∪∪....... s dressed up madness." Notman accused Jason and his
ilk of treason for tearing the country apart for no discernible reason, for
unleashing irrationality and violence and destruction on a scale they
couldn't possibly harness. Jason was taking it no more.

"I see you don't get the point, even when you've had a chance to convert
in your final hours. You know what I despise most about you, William?
You and your kind are weak. No one cares about facts or your patheti-
cally weak liberal notions of redistributing my wealth for your puny
programs that do nothing but encourage laziness and sloth. When it
comes down to it, no one important cares about rights or diversity or
saving this orb from environmental destruction. If destruction is Galt's
will, don't fight it; embrace it, we say, and make the best money-making
opportunity you can. Your arrogant and condescending liberalism was
the path to quick decline. We believe in the inevitability of tragedy and
if millions of moochers and takers starve and die or are killed in a just
war, then let them bleed. They are a drain and won't be missed just as
they are never missed when histories are written.

"You don't know or read your own history. This country was found-
ed on the basis of inequality and the Galtian Imperatives represent the
dawn of a new and Real American civilization built on the inequality
of our forefathers. This country had gone soft and economic terror was
required to toughen it up. We have destroyed your soft stage of democracy and are building a new one for coming generations of genius who
won't be detoured."

Notman didn't offer a direct rebuttal to what he, Jason, considered a
brilliant dissertation. As he struggled through the drug-induced haze as

the crowd at Final Justice Stadium cheered loudly in the background, Jason remembered that Notman smiled and shook his head.

"Jason, you're a true believer which makes you naïve and deadly at the same time. You want to convert me and embrace these silly imperatives that no one understands. From my perspective, the perspective of an innocent man who will be executed so others may profit, this is an absurd moment and you can't see it. I will read my script to protect my family but let's be clear. I know your madness is a fever that can't be controlled and if this is my fate, then so be it. I would watch out Jason, because your kind has unleashed a destructive force you can't control and I suspect you won't be around much longer than me. This may be cliché but revolutions devour their own creators rather easily and quickly. You will die a fool."

Notman was right, Jason thought, as he heard the stadium crowd react with boos and jeers to his vidconfession of Real American treason and extensive anti-Galtian activities. Revolutions do devour their own but Notman, as usual, had missed the point because I, Jason Bravtart, will be sacrificed for a great cause, to let the Galtian Imperatives live and prosper. I, Jason Bravtart, will die a patriot and a genius.

Making perfect sense

Due to his death, Jason would miss Bowie's major press conference scheduled for the next day. The leader of the New Southern Alliance was scheduled to announce "serious negotiations with our friends in the Northern Confederation" to expand Execution Channel franchise rights to more states and to a growing international market. The two alliances also were expected to announce joint steps to "eliminate first the reality and eventually the idea of government" by the year 2045. News was also leaked that Bowie was seeking an architect to design the first "Austerity Monument" park in Real America.

"We want it to symbolize the importance of ignoring history and embracing destruction and austerity for no reason except than it should be done. We feel such a monument consisting of nothing will show the true essence of the Galtian Imperatives and be an inspiration to all Real Americans and our Guardians of Galt," said Roland Gunner, Bowie's new chief of staff and CEO of the renamed Bowie Empire Enterprises.

Later that week, Bowie said that BEE would buy the remaining elements of the Real American Republic of Texas government. Bowie would pocket a 1.5 million RAC genius fee for selling the state he was elected to lead to the company he had acquired in a hostile takeover. BEE had written and paid for an editorial in the Galt Street Journal that concluded "This dismantling of government merger represents a triumph of free market ingenuity and further evidence of the undeniable logic of the Galtian imperatives."

In addition to the increased execution schedule to celebrate the Galt Week holiday, Bowie would also announce a book and televinet deal to tell "the inspiring real story behind the worldwide, moneymaking success and genius of the Execution Channel." More than a dozen scribes working for BEE had written feverishly over the past 24 hours to create an alternative past for which Bowie would receive a 4.5 million RAC advance. They were using material provided willingly by Jason during his interrogations with Jones' agents and then revising it to fit with the new story line that showed Bowie as the rightful genius behind the Execution Channel. In the first edition, Jason's role would be reduced to a mere footnote of public relations consultation and it would eliminated altogether in later versions. But Jason would go down in the record books as the highest rated execution of 2018.

Gov. Bowie's press office also released a statement saying that the rumored war between the Real American Republic of Texas and Mexico was being averted and a "peace and prosperity" conference had been scheduled to discuss Execution Channel franchise rights. The press release also said that Bowie was negotiating a cease fire to stop the ongoing civil conflict in California. "There may come a time when it becomes economically necessary to restart the war but we hope to persuade our non-Galtian neighbors to negotiate in good faith and give us what we want," Bowie said.

The press office held back news for a week on the pending sale of the Execution Channel to an international group of private equity investors for 59 billion Australian Dollars (the new preferred currency of international transactions). The sale amount was 500 million AD below what Gunner and the boys in the BEE number-crunching shop had predicted was the top of the Execution Channel bubble.

As Jason's vidconfession came to end, Penelope watched on televinet from Canada and Bowie watched from the governor's special luxury box as the lights went out and the spotlight was focused on Jason as he walked into the stadium, escorted by two scantily dressed women who waved at the crowd. There was a cascade of boos and calls of "traitor to Galt" and "looter" and "collectivator."

Three black-clad men were then spotlighted and they waved to the cheering fans as they walked to the .50-caliber machine guns they would soon fire. The bullets would tear Jason to shreds and kill him instantly, but the latest in slow-motion vidmaterial upgrades would provide plenty of execution replays of flying blood trails and a shattered body. Jason was securely bound by extra strong ropes, which would keep him upright until his body began to fall apart from the machine gun volleys. As the crowd reacted with fever pitch cheers, the public address announcer read the warrant charges, the tribunal sentence and the guilty verdict of Execution Channel death.

Then came a ritual established with the first ExSub William Notman. A voice filled the stadium with John Galt's words from *Atlas Shrugged*.

"Yes, this is an age of moral crisis. Yes, you are bearing punishment for your evil. But it is not man who is now on trial and it is not human nature that will take the blame. It is your moral code that is through this time."

After the reverential collective hush from the audience, the next part of the festivities came right on cue. Jason saw and heard his redemptive declaration on the vidconfession screen: "I have been impure and done serious wrong to our cause by giving aid and comfort to our enemies. I repent before my end and declare this to be a glorious moment. I fell from the true path but I urge you, you Real American patriots, to stay true and embrace the dawn of the great Real American civilization. Long live John Galt! Long live the Execution Channel! Long live Real America! Long live the Galtian Imperatives!"

There was a mix of cheers and jeers from the fans in the stands. Penelope had never met Jason but felt tied to him somehow. Nothing that happened in Real America surprised her anymore but she felt a slight regret about Jason and how she had helped set him up. Penelope could not watch the execution and was beginning to turn away from the televinet screen when a close up camera shot showed Jason smiling. She wondered about the source of the smile and what Jason was thinking.

The smile reflected a flash of cosmic symmetry. Jason had seen the flashing number 347 on one of the large digital displays inside the stadium just as he heard the cocking of the machine guns. 347. He realized he was a few seconds away from being confirmed ExSub 347 in the Execution Channel count of ExSubs. The ExSub count number flashed until the ExSub was dead and was no longer a potential ExSub but a confirmed one and then the flashing would stop. 347. Sometime later, in another state that very night, there would be an ExSub 348 but Jason was 347.

Despite the drugs taking maximum effect, he discovered a clear neural connection and sensed a burst of fragments, a collage of the daily waking up at exactly 3:47 a.m. during his exile. 347 represented despair and then triumphant breakthrough. And now it represented death, his death. 347. It was he who gave the Execution Channel life and now he was ExSub 347. Jason had one last burst of mental clarity before the three mercenaries fired the first of three, two-second machine gun volleys. 347. It all makes perfect sense, he thought. I can circle a square.

Paradise at hand

Six weeks after the execution of ExSub 347, the Execution Channel investment bubble burst and it sent the fragmented country's economy into a devastating tailspin. Private investors, large banks, and hedge fund managers quickly demanded help from the few remaining non-privatized, cash-strapped states to cover their investment losses.

"It must be done to protect our Guardians of Galt from the harsh reality of failure and shield them from their own folly. We need to boost their morale for the hard days ahead," said the Galt Street Journal in support of the bailouts. Though various parts of the Real America were now declared "high depression zones" and considered beyond economic rescue, the editorial said it was not time to change course.

Lawrence C. Bowie, the new owner and CEO of the New Southern Alliance, called on Real American patriots to stiffen their spines. Bowie Empire Enterprises had purchased the 20-state New Southern Alliance two weeks after the bubble burst for an undisclosed amount. Bowie appointed new proconsuls and legislators for each of the newly named Liberty Republics, an innovation he said would eliminate the "dead-weight inefficiencies of democracy" and unleash the Galtian Imperatives "once and for all."

In a televinet address to Real American, Bowie urged patience and diligence. "This economic downturn is but a minor setback and shows that our methods are working. Mama Bowie says this is a test of our will and frankly, our resolve to eliminate government and let freedom ring has never been stronger. We cannot abandon austerity measures that have proven to work splendidly in tandem with unquestioned obedience to the Galtian Imperatives. Our Guardians of Galt stand united and state unequivocally that paradise is close at hand."

The End

Made in the USA
Lexington, KY
24 July 2013